"I interviewed Ron and Glenda Pettey about Ron's experience in Heaven. His is one of the most authentic and revelatory experiences I've encountered.

Now that Ron is in Heaven, his wife is releasing the rest of the revelation . . ."

—Sid Roth,
Host, *It's Supernatural!* television

"The Petteys' story is about the perseverance to believe for a miracle in the face of seemingly insurmountable obstacles. But, even more importantly, it's a story of the unfailing power of God's word and the humble practice of living out the patience that comes from true marital devotion. You will believe that love truly bears up under all, hopes all, believes all, conquers all—love wins!"

—David Kithcart
Features Director, The 700 Club

"I am honored to recommend this special book. Together, both Ron and Glenda overcame obstacles with a grace and power that can only be called supernatural. I've been the recipient of Ron's incredible discernment, loving counsel and X-ray vision. He was a person living in the Kingdom of God, even as he sat talking with someone in a busy restaurant. I'm excited about this book, the adventure it holds, and the wisdom it shares. Read it and you'll see why."

—The Rev. Joseph K. Acton
Senior Pastor
Rancho Vineyard Church, San Diego, CA

"Near-death experiences fascinate us. Having "been there, done that" myself, I now have no fear of death. To know the hope in death is comforting. St. Paul even wrote about it: 'I know a man who was caught up to the third Heaven, whether in body or out of body, I don't know.' Paul, like Ron and Glenda, told his story, but in the third person. I recommend this book as a resource for your earthly journey."

—The Rev. Nigel W.D. Mumford,
author of *Dying to Live*

"Just wanted to say thank you for praying for us last night, and the word of knowledge given to Bro. Ron for our health. I went into Conway this morning and got apple cider vinegar as well as plain apple cider. I read online last night that apple cider vinegar is good for all types of skin conditions including psoriasis, and circulation problems, too. Bro. Ron was right on in his word of knowledge! UPDATE, After 2.5 weeks: The transformation on my psoriasis is a miracle! It is almost all healed with no new outbreak areas. Also, my puffy right ankle is improving every day. My pain factor is zero! It's a miracle from God and I give Him ALL the glory. GOD IS GOOD ALL THE TIME! I'm so thrilled by what He has done for me!"

—Jan England, Arkansas

"Our 17-year-old son, Michael, had been feeling sick for a few days, so I let him stay home from school. By Friday evening, he was hurting so badly that he could not sit or lie down comfortably. I realized we needed to go to the emergency room. So the first thing I did was to pray. The second thing I did was call Ron and Glenda Pettey. They offered to meet us at the entrance to the ER. Michael's pain was so intense that I had to put his shoes and socks on for him. While helping him, I asked God why this was happening. Our insurance was due to kick in one week from that day. The Lord gave me a peace, so we went forward. As we turned off our road headed for the hospital, a thought came to me. I asked Michael if he had been having blood in his urine. He had. (Why had he not told me?) I realized it was kidney stones. When we arrived at the hospital, I told Ron and Glenda my thoughts and Ron confirmed them. He told me that there were three stones and that they were gone! I almost shouted. I did thank God, and Ron and Glenda. Michael went to the bathroom at the hospital and passed the stones. Thank God that the waiting room was the only part of the hospital we needed that night. For the next several days, he had symptoms of a person who had passed kidney stones (according to a friend who had the experience a few times). This is only one of the times my family and I have been blessed by Ron and Glenda's ministry. I thank God for them and recommend them to anyone needing a healing miracle."

—Debbie Reed, Lufkin, TX

"Thank you for praying for our elderly friend Sis Eva Enriquez while you visited the Christ Healing Center in San Antonio in July. She had been experiencing a severe pain on the lower left side of her body and had been taking 500 mg. of hydrocodone twice a day. The night she went home after you prayed for her she did not take the medication. The next day, again she did not take it in the morning. The pain was completely gone! Praise be to the Lord and thank you both for your love and faithfulness to the Lord and His people. May the Lord continue to work miracles through you!"

—Polly Marin, San Antonio, TX

"It was life-changing to meet you both and see how God is working through and in each of you. Sometimes we become dead to the power and wonders, and our meeting truly renewed me in every sense of the word. I am still reeling in my new freedom and feel light and encouraged. I really needed confirmation on the astrology and Mary and the saints. Out of despair, I was really reaching. I hope you will publish a prayer book some day! I will continue to put one foot in front of the other and TRUST in HIM! I am in the process of reading and sharing your book! Don't be surprised if you see me at some of your gatherings!"

—Jennifer, Texas

"I want to share an amazing testimony of the Lord's goodness and healing power! I connected with Ron and Glenda by phone for prayer in December of 2009, it was an amazing time! God revealed to Ron that there was a condition concerning my heart. Glenda and I were going through some prayers, and I could feel God's healing power come upon me as we were praying . . . I could feel heat, a warm sensation, in different areas of my body, specifically where Ron had sensed a problem regarding the arteries by my heart. Later on that same night after talking with Ron and Glenda, I could feel cooling sensations all throughout my body . . . the pent-up emotions were being released that were affecting the functions of my heart, and the blood flow and circulation were getting better! In fact, weeks went by and even over a month later I could still feel God's healing power! Praise God! I believe that God is continuing to heal me as I choose to forgive completely. God is so amazing! God was doing surgery on me right there in my home! With God all things are possible! God can and wants to heal you . . . just believe and have faith in Him! Put your hope in God . . . it is amazing what He can do! Thank you so much Ron and Glenda for praying with me! Ron, the Lord has given you such an amazing gift of healing! Thank you so much Glenda for your prayers and words of encouragement! Praise be to God!"

—Kimberly, Minnesota

"I had diarrhea for over two weeks and had become severely dehydrated. On the Sunday just before I had finally decided to go the doctor, I met Ron in our church foyer and asked for prayer. Ron prayed for everything to simply line up in my body. "Jesus, align everything in his body according to the way You designed it." There was no shock wave, no fanfare, no thunder and lightning . . . Just a simple 10-second prayer. Later that day, I realized that I had no need to rush the restroom as I had done for so many days. I was instantly normal! No need for the doctor! The debilitating condition has never returned. Glory to God! What a Glorious God we serve!"

—**Robert Blanton**, Lufkin, TX

"I just wanted to thank you both for praying for my daughter, Morgan, on March 17. She was having severe seizures prior to that time, even with medication. During her last seizure in February I asked the Lord why this was happening. He told me "this kind only comes out with prayer and fasting." So, I immediately started fasting. Then we met with you all in March, and I am happy to report that she has had no problems since you prayed! UPDATE: Not only has she had no problems since you prayed, but we went to her neurologist today (9-23-10) and the EEG was repeated—the results are NORMAL!!!!!! PRAISE GOD!!!! This confirms the miracle that took place in March 2009. Thanks so much for all you do!"

—**Selena Hester Elliott**, Mansfield, TX

". . . finally a moment to reflect on last weekend's powerful message and experience of healing. What a blessing to have met you both. Your story is so powerful and the reasons God had you return from Heaven, Ron, are obvious!!!! Healing in my body seems complete and the heart continues to heal. Thank you so much for your boldness and perseverance in writing and sharing your story and your gift of healing!"

—**H. Fraser**, Houston, Texas

"The Lord had started moving on us prior to your arrival and in His wisdom He used you to build on what He was doing. Since you left so much has happened. The Lord is really moving, healing people's hearts, minds and bodies. It is very exciting to see how He is moving and we can't wait to receive more and more revelation from Him."

—**Cheryl Ray**, Prayer Coordinator,
New Haven House of Prayer, The Woodlands, TX

"When you prayed for me in June, one of my health issues was low thyroid. I had been off my medication since January because I had a bad reaction to it, and I was afraid that by June, my thyroid would be totally "out of whack." I went in for some blood work about a month after you prayed for me, and my TSH score, which is the indicator of the thyroid level, was 6.9, only a little above normal (anything above 5.5 indicates low thyroid). This was really good news, because the last time I went off my medication, my level got up to 75. Then last week I was tested again, and my TSH was at 5.7! I am praising and thanking God, because this has to be some kind of miracle. My doctor is happy with my results, and says I don't need to be on the medication. Thank you again for your prayers, and thank you Jesus for healing me!!"

—**Beth Banks**, Houston, TX

"I came before Christmas '08 for Ron to pray for me after my motorcycle accident. I started healing immediately after four months of going nowhere. Totally healed! Glory to Jesus! Thanks for your gift. Charge on and Bless the People!"

—**J. Paterson**, Stephenville, TX

"I had been diagnosed with hepatitis C in 1991. When I met Ron and Glenda in May 2008, I asked them to pray for my elevated liver enzymes. A month later my blood work showed that the viral count had gone down. The constant pain on my right side significantly diminished. But even more wonderful was how marvelously and discreetly the Lord healed me of incontinence that had developed after the birth of my fourth child and had grown worse years later after child number five. I did not mention this condition to them: only the Lord knew! The surgery that I was considering is no longer needed. I am completely healed of this annoying and debilitating condition . . . Praise God!"

—**Marnie Woodyard**, Abilene, Texas

"I saw your video on Sid Roth/Youtube. This was such a great interview of you two. I'm originally from Center, Texas and I grew up with Scotty Hennigan in First Baptist Church. He was three years older than me in school. I laughed when you said that he looked at you and said, "I got into Heaven and you didn't." That is just like him. I've always been quick on my feet but I was no match for him in wits. He was quick. He was a very sick young man but his spirits were always up. I'm glad to hear he is in a better place. Thanks for your testimony. It's a blessing. God Bless You!"

—**Jonathan Hopkins**, The Colony, TX

"During a recent visit with Ron & Glenda Pettey, I received healing for a heart condition that I had been diagnosed with over a year ago. This condition's side effects included: tiredness, pain and slow blood flow that went in reverse around the heart. I started having intense pain on the right side of my chest. Through prayer and the gifts of healing that God has given Ron, Ron correctly diagnosed my heart condition and prayed for the Lord to relieve the pain and correct the blood flow in and around my heart. Prior to receiving this prayer, I struggled with tiredness that overwhelmed me during the week. After receiving prayer, I notice a marked improvement in my energy level that continues to grow day after day. I thank The Lord for His mercy and grace and for gifting Ron and Glenda Pettey with these healing gifts. The Lord is using them to bring His holy healing to the body of Christ and to needy people everywhere. Praise be to Jesus!"

—**M. Murrell**, Houston, Texas

"In May 2005, my 13-year-old old daughter, Morgan, started having slight nausea and stomach pain. During the summer, she started losing weight and becoming very weak. Her diagnosis after many tests was H-pylori, a bacteria that can cause ulcers in the stomach. Our doctor put her on a regimen of Biaxin and Pepto-Bismol multiple times a day, with a bland diet. She was cured after an entire summer of weakness and weight loss. However, in the fall she kept complaining of stomachaches. Being somewhat shell-shocked, I became anxious that something was still wrong. Although our doctor assured us that she was OK, he agreed to order her a stomach scope. The day before this test we visited Ron and Glenda to purchase their book "Heaven is Real" and to ask them to pray for her. Morgan told me later that she felt something tingly in her stomach while they prayed. The next day the doctor scoped her stomach and told us that not only was her stomach completely healed, but also there was no evidence of scar tissue from her past ulcer. I believe in my heart that the Lord healed my daughter through prayer. We praise the Lord for this complete healing in our daughter."

—**C. Cook**, Nacogdoches, Texas

"I have had back pain on and off for more than ten years. You prayed for my back on Sunday and I am completely amazed at how my back has felt for the past two days. It feels like you pulled 50 pounds off of my lower back! I have never had such an experience before. I thank God for you two and am praising the Father for my blessing."

—**B. Ross**, Lufkin, Texas

Heaven is Real . . .
The Rest of the Story

by Ron & Glenda Pettey

Cover painting "Sunrise with Cirrus Clouds"
by Howard Storm

Published by

 köehlerbooks™

210 60th Street
Virginia Beach, VA 23451
800-435-4811
www.koehlerbooks.com

HEAVEN IS REAL

... *the rest of the story*

Ron & Glenda Pettey

VIRGINIA BEACH
CAPE CHARLES

CONTENTS

PART ONE:

PART TWO:

PART I

1998

FOREWORD

By Wanda Pridgeon

What would it be like to arrive at the gate of Heaven and be turned back? How would you feel if you had glimpsed the perfection awaiting you, and then you were told to re-enter your pain-ridden, earthly body? And on top of that, how would you cope with life without the ability to remember? Ron Pettey can answer these questions. He's been to Heaven and back and then lived ten years without an earthly memory.

My first meeting with Ron and Glenda Pettey was at an interview for my work as a writer for a Christian newspaper. My husband, Les, an ordained Baptist minister, accompanied me. We had heard about Ron's out-of-body experience and were prepared to dismiss it as someone's vivid imagination or wild dream. We certainly were not prepared for what we heard.

Ron is a tall, slender man with a happy face. If he isn't actually smiling, there is an inward joy radiating from his eyes. As he began to tell us of his experiences, we sensed a genuineness that could not be denied.

Our doubts were replaced with a conviction that this man is a recipient of a true miracle. Les' response of tears that day validated for me Ron's story. We spoke often of the positive impact Ron's and Glenda's experiences have had on our lives. Because we believed those experiences would affect others in the same way, Les (before his death a few months later) repeatedly encouraged me to write their story.

Thank you, Lord, for the privilege and honor of being a part of this effort.

It is our sincere prayer that you will allow the Holy Spirit of God to use this message to change your life.

Christians, rejoice—Heaven is real!

If you are not yet a believer in Christ, please know that the WAY to Heaven is just as real. *"For whosoever shall call upon the name of the Lord shall be saved"* (Romans 10:13).

INTRODUCTION

By Ron

The sound of the doorbell was a welcome diversion to an otherwise uneventful summer morning in 1995. Mr. Best, our new mail carrier, was at the door. He asked, "Is this the home of the man who has seen Heaven and had miracles in his life?"

"Yes, you have the right house!" I said.

Best had heard a cassette recording of my testimony the night before. A co-worker had bought a box of tapes at a rummage sale and as he played and sorted them, he found my testimony. This tape made the rounds until finally Best got his turn. "My wife and I were captivated the entire hour as we listened to your story," he said.

The message Best was excited about was of my incredible journey to Heaven and back in 1982.

In Heaven I was introduced to my guardian angel. Later in my hospital room, the angel gently cautioned me to be slow in sharing this testimony. Weeks later I came to understand that *slow* meant to be cautious—to wait for God's direction. From one-on-one to small groups to congregations, the opportunities began to come. Eventually I spoke on radio and television.

Now, after more than fifteen years, the Lord is directing the writing of this book. In it, although we have changed some names to protect the privacy of the individuals, Glenda and I sense that God is ready to enlarge His audience. May you be richly blessed as you walk with us through the experiences that God gave us and commissioned us to share.

CHAPTER 1

ENCOUNTER
WITH DESTINY

By Ron

"**W**hat do you mean that my name is not in the book? I have done everything necessary to be allowed into Heaven! Look again!" I commanded the gentleman behind the check-in table in the foyer of Heaven.*

At age thirty-three, married and the father of two, I believed in Jesus and trusted Him for my eternal home. Death took me by complete surprise. An even greater surprise was that my name was not found in the admission book to Heaven. I thank the Lord that He didn't take me on that journey a few years earlier—I probably wouldn't be around now to tell you about it. Experiencing God's love made all the difference. Let me explain how that transition came about.

On a 1973 spring visit to my sister in West Texas my life was to be forever changed.

I had lived my teen and early adult years in opposition to God. My upbringing in church and home was solid, but I was running in the wrong direction. My family was frustrated and deeply concerned. Willing to try anything, my sister Nell arranged a blind date with Glenda, a girl from her church. Unknown to me was the *briefing* Glenda received before our evening out.

My sister advised me to escort Glenda to a respectable restaurant (without a bar), see a G-rated movie and be on my best behavior. I almost melted on the front porch as I caught my first glimpse of her coming to the door. This was a blind date like no other! The perky coed with shoulder-length golden brown hair and sparkling blue eyes greeted me with a genuine smile. "This is too good to be true!" I thought.

We dined at a stylish restaurant in San Angelo where the salad bar was years ahead of its time. The musical comedy, "1776," was a hit and only too soon I was driving her home. Instead of saying goodbye, Glenda hesitated to leave the car. She awkwardly asked, "Ron, does your life have purpose and meaning?" As I was thinking about how to answer her, this beautiful young woman began telling me of her Savior and how He could be mine, too. The Lord used her quiet spirit and compassionate words to make me realize how empty my life was. Deep within I knew that Jesus was the only answer. I hardly remembered my baptism as a twelve-year-old in our large Baptist church. I had given in to the wrong role models and peer pressure as a youth. Eventually, smoking, drinking beer, and gambling over games of golf and poker had become part of my lifestyle. The guilt I sensed was real. Now, for the first time, I felt like God himself was speaking to me and I welcomed His voice! I suddenly knew that my life would be meaningless to continue without Him. For twenty-three years I had tried to find happiness in entertainment, nice cars and clothes—the trappings that only money could buy. Now, I knew Jesus was the *only* way. Without hesitation I prayed with Glenda and asked Jesus to be my Lord and Savior.

With a new spirit, I was drawn to Glenda's radiant countenance. "Could I see you tomorrow?" I asked. My heart leaped with joy when she said, "Yes, I'd love it."

Driving back to my sister's house, I tossed my new, expensive lighter along with a pack of cigarettes into a dumpster. The joy and freedom I had was incredible. I woke Nell and knelt at her bedside to tell her my exciting news. She had no idea how profoundly her prayers had been answered.

GLENDA'S ACCOUNT OF THE MEETING

"Yes," I answered the soft voice on the phone, "I'd be glad to meet your brother and go out this Saturday night, and I'll do what I can to tell him about Jesus." I hung up with my heart pounding, feeling I had just signed up for a foreign mission assignment. Here I was—twenty-one years old with a near-perfect attendance record in church, present for every class, choir and program that was ever held and now I was to actually tell someone the good news of Christ! "At least he's from East Texas and only here for a short visit; if I blow it, chances are I'll never see him again," I consoled myself.

I was pleasantly surprised to see such a tall, nice looking *older* man (after all, he was almost twenty-four). I soon found that his manners were impeccable—opening doors, ordering for me, showing refinement in every way. The meal and movie were delightful and before I knew it, I felt like the Cinderella clock was ticking. I was hoping for a fast-food soft drink to buy more time. Instead, the car stopped at my house. With all the small talk exhausted, in the seconds that remained I took a silent, deep breath and blurted out something about God giving me purpose in my life. To my amazement, Ron was sincerely interested. Although I was numb to the entire conversation, I kept smiling and trusting the Lord to speak through me. I was awed that Ron was ready to ask God for forgiveness and receive the free gift of eternal life. I guided him through a simple prayer. When I opened my eyes, Ron's face was beaming and he began talking about Jesus now being the Lord of his life. He was at once serious about his new faith. I relaxed and knew Nell would be pleased. From my background, I knew that angels in Heaven were rejoicing over another person's believing. My mission was successful and I wouldn't even mind seeing the fellow from East Texas again.

Mr. and Mrs. J. B. Stricklin
request the honour of your presence
at the marriage of their daughter
Glenda Sue
to
Mr. Ronald Everett Petty
on Saturday, the twenty-sixth of May
nineteen hundred and seventy-three
at seven o'clock in the evening
First Baptist Church Chapel
San Angelo, Texas

RON CONTINUES

Next day, as we strolled along a beautiful river walk in San Angelo, I began to realize some major changes had taken place in me. For one thing, all I wanted to talk about was God's love and His plan for my life. For another, I had no more desire for cigarettes and alcohol. I didn't even want to be on the golf course across the street. I was a new creation!

By the end of the evening, I felt I had known Glenda my entire life. Laughter punctuated our conversation and before the second day was over we were making wedding plans.

I called my parents and announced, "Cancel my golf cart order and send the money! I need to buy a *ring*! . . . I have so much to tell you." I would wait to tell them face to face that their prayers had been answered, that Jesus was now my Savior and Lord. My life would never be the same.

Returning home, I embraced my parents—they could see the change in my face. The next Sunday my pastor met me halfway down the aisle as I bolted at the first opportunity to make my decision for Christ known to my church.

Glenda finished her last semester of college amid the flurry of wedding arrangements. Our parents met and instantly liked each other. Every detail rapidly came into place. We found that with God *all* things are indeed possible.

From a blind date through a whirlwind courtship and storybook wedding, Glenda and I began an exciting journey toward learning to experience God in His fullness.

As a married man with new responsibilities, I needed to return to college to finish my business degree. In two years I graduated and Sears hired me as a manager in their catalog division. After training and several transfers, I became the store manager of the Sears store in Port Lavaca, a small town on the Texas coast.

During these honeymoon years, Glenda taught school and I ran the store. However, to Glenda's chagrin, I sensed the Lord directing me to enter the ministry. Despite her strong faith, she refused to discuss the possibility. She argued, "The Lord needs Christian businessmen and I do not feel the call to be a pastor's wife!" I would drop the subject for another several months.

We both wanted to start a family, and as time passed, we grew concerned that it wasn't happening. Month after month our hope faded with negative results. Soon we were deeply frustrated and had to put this desire aside, until Evangelist Cliff Brannon and his wife, Ruth, led a week-long revival at our church.

One evening Ruth shared her testimony of how she had resented her husband's lay-preaching ministry. She related: "One of our children became critically ill. As the hours of life were slipping away from our precious child, I realized that it was my own resistance to the Lord that was blocking her recovery. I cried out in repentance to God and gave Cliff over to Him. I submitted to be content with the Lord's plan. My child's fever suddenly began to drop and everyone witnessed a miraculous recovery."

Glenda identified with Ruth's crisis and later that evening admitted, "I now understand why a blessing of a child is being withheld." She shocked me when she stepped out to meet our pastor at the end of the service. She confessed, "I have resisted God's working in our lives and I'm releasing Ron to answer His call."

Elated over this new freedom to follow the Lord, I received a minister's license through our church and wise counsel about how to prepare a sermon. In the weeks to come, I filled pulpits in several small country churches. Within a calendar year, we held our firstborn, Jennifer, in our arms! God is so good!

1978 was a milestone year for us. With the birth of our first child and my Sears transfer to Alvin, a suburb of Houston, Glenda became a mother-at-home. Without her salary as a teacher, our income was significantly reduced. After the move, my eagerness to preach seemed to fall on deaf ears. No calls came. Our attention was then diverted to starting a home business. The intent was to make up for the financial deficit while Glenda stayed at home. In hindsight, we acknowledge that the business fostered an independent spirit in us. Our focus shifted from looking to the Lord to meet our needs to relying on our own efforts. This was the beginning of trouble for us. Because the business required total involvement from both of us, we had little time for each other. For the first time in our marriage, we became argumentative and competitive. Even though we appeared to achieve a measure of success, our debts grew and our relationship with our Heavenly Father suffered.

In the fall of that year I began to have headaches. After several months of medical tests, I was diagnosed with hydrocephalus, a condition caused by failure of the spinal fluid to drain properly from the brain to the spinal column. Brain surgery was my only option. In December the doctors installed a valve and a plastic tube (shunt) in my head to correct the pressure. I returned to my Sears desk in record time.

In June of '79 we passed another milestone. We learned that Christians are not exempt from the tragedies of life. When she was seven weeks from her delivery date with our second child, Glenda was forced by pain to leave a church function. She said she could not imagine what was going wrong with her body. I was home on my first day of retirement from Sears to devote my attention to our home business.

I rushed Glenda to the hospital. Our first son, Jason,

was stillborn. God was pressing us into maturity with Him. The baby's medical exam showed nothing physically wrong, leaving us without answers. We experienced unspeakable pain. The recovery process was a healing that only God Himself could give. Only the Lord's grace and peace that passes all understanding carried us through that time.

My health was normal until the summer of 1981 when I disturbed the shunt tubing while teaching my young daughter to swim. I had three brain surgeries that summer to correct it. Glenda survived that six-week period and remembers it as our time in the emergency room with the "revolving door."

If this wasn't enough, on a weekend in October strange sensations overtook my body. An insatiable thirst for liquids could not quench my cotton dry mouth. Trauma diabetes, caused by the string of surgeries, was not news I wanted to hear. For three weeks I was again in the hospital getting my insulin dosages and diet under control when the Lord arranged an unusual blessing of setting me up in diabetic research. So, over the next few years I donated a week at a time for hospital testing in exchange for my diabetic supplies. Grateful for the excellent professional care, I found God had allowed me to be at the forefront of medical developments.

In March of 1982 God blessed us with our second daughter, Kimberly. Remarkably, my health improved enough to allow me to assist Glenda with all the aspects of parenting until July. It was then that my shunt failed again. This time I had developed a slow-growing infection and the shunt had to be replaced.

Optimistic about full recovery, I was eager to get the surgery over with. Thank goodness we didn't know what trials lay ahead. During the removal process, a massive blood clot formed on my brain and was not detected by

X-ray. Without realizing it, the doctors inserted the tubing into this clot and it could not drain. However, the surgery was an *apparent* success; days passed before the effects of the error would be known.

By Saturday evening the pressure on my brain had built to the explosion level. Glenda sensed that the shunt was not functioning, but the medical staff would not listen. Although my face was swollen beyond recognition, the doctors assured her they had merely hit a gland.

At 6 a.m. the next morning (Sunday) I was rushed back into surgery. The prognosis was grim.

CHAPTER TWO

GOD'S MERCY DEMONSTRATED

By Glenda

The weekend hours drudged by. I felt fatigue setting in on the lonesome drive home from the Houston VA hospital late Saturday. Physically and emotionally exhausted, I mumbled a greeting to my family and went straight to my room. No longer able to contain my grief, I collapsed on my bed. In anger and defeat I prayed and wept into the night. Fearful of Ron's death, I finally faced the reality of becoming a young widow with two small children to raise. In the midst of my suffering, I could no longer hang on to Ron. All my positive thinking and praying was spent. In desperation, I released him to God with no strings attached. Just as I formed the words in my mouth, "Lord, he's yours," I audibly heard God's voice: "I'm giving him back, he's going to be OK!" Wow! The unmistakable presence of the Lord dried my tears and restful sleep came!

One shrill ring woke me at 6 a.m.—I grabbed the phone. The doctor's voice was somehow not a surprise. "In making our early morning rounds, we've discovered Ron's spinal fluid is not draining. We're preparing him for surgery now," he said. "Come as soon as you can; we need your signature."

God's peace was with me as I dashed to the hospital that Sunday morning. The chief neurosurgeon offered little hope as I signed the medical release forms one more time. With the surgery underway, I began to collect my thoughts and realized it was Sunday. Family and friends were just waking and would soon be leaving for church. Finding a phone, I placed calls across the state. "I need your help to pray for Ron right now, and please ask your pastor to mention his name to the congregation." With the strength of God I was able to calmly explain the crisis and ask each one to bring this urgent request before the Lord during their church services.

The family began gathering in the now-familiar surgical waiting room. Hours passed with no word from the doctor. We tried to pray, re-read *Guideposts*, even work jigsaw puzzles. No one was interested in the array of snacks; we had had our fill of coffee. Past lunchtime, a young man from our church burst into the room. Steve's countenance shone with hope and joy as he shared his message: "During the worship service and prayer for Ron, I sensed the Lord telling me that Ron was going to be OK and that I was to come tell you." My spirit soared with this confirmation of my own "message!" Steve humbly confessed, "I really questioned making the long drive with my family to the medical center and even went halfway home when the Lord made me turn the car around and come. Please forgive me for delaying." Then he said, "Let's form a circle and praise the Lord for what He is already doing." Though some of us were reluctant at first, we cooperated and in the course of his prayer we were encouraged.

As the prayer ended, I realized that the doctor was waiting to see me. He explained the severity of Ron's condition. "There is extreme pressure in his brain that may take days to correct," he said. "And we don't know the effect on Ron's vision, personality, memory, and even his ultimate survival!"

Somewhat detached, I said, "Thank you for your effort and concern. I know you and the staff are doing the best you can." My peaceful smile must have indicated that I seemed oblivious to his report. He nodded cordially to the rest of the family and slipped out of the room. Steve then reaffirmed the divine word from God. Hand in hand, the family again prayed, this time much more fervently than before. Steve prayed, "Lord, thank you for the doctors and their abilities, but we are standing on *Your* revelation to us that *You* have Ron's life under control and that he will be OK."

Originally fearful that Ron might not even awaken from the surgery, the doctor was back in twenty-five minutes. "Would you like to see him now?" he asked. Pinned under a maze of monitors and IV lines and so very frail, Ron responded. He was still with us. What a victory—God was in control!

Abounding hope continued in the days and weeks that followed. My own relationship with Jesus was more beautiful and precious than ever before. I had so much to be thankful for: for my mother's strength to keep the children, for supernaturally holding the Houston traffic back as I traveled and even for the parking places He always opened for me in the crowded lot. I began to pray for other patients and their families as I saw them in the hallways. Then, most profoundly, He taught me to pray for mercy for Ron's recovery. I grew to feel that the healing I wanted so much for my husband was completely undeserved and unmerited. Ron's sister, Nell, agreed with me and we found ourselves pleading desperately for mercy during the short visiting sessions we had with him.

Then a strange thing happened. During one visit, Ron tried to introduce Nell and me to an invisible person. He pointed beyond the right foot of his bed and insisted, "I want you to meet this gentleman." We looked into the empty space and sadly turned back to each other. "Can't you see him?" he demanded. "He's right there."

Trying to appease him, Nell suggested, "Do you mean the doctor?"

"What about your male nurse?" I added.

"Surely, you aren't pointing to another patient?" we pleaded.

Ron became more and more frustrated with our obstinacy. "Honey, there's no one there," I said, trying to coax him back to reality. His parents and nephew took their turns at his bedside. We feared the hallucinations were signaling a permanent setback. Not until another couple of visits at the four-hour intervals did Ron finally drop the issue. We sighed a deep relief.

Ron slowly gained strength. After a week of observing the spinal fluid in an external drain, the doctors were ready to place the tubing inside and finish the procedure. This time all went well.

On the last day of August, 1982, Ron's parents and I brought him home to greet his children whom he had not seen in six weeks.

In the hospital I assumed Ron knew me, although he had not recognized the children from pictures. I was naive to think that he would improve and the effects of the surgery would clear in time. Ron's memory was indeed impaired and daily he would have to find a way to cope with the simplest aspects of life.

A week after coming home from the hospital, Ron lay awake in bed and began to speak with deep conviction, "Glenda, I have taken a trip."

I tried to humor him by saying, "Yes, you had quite a long stay at the Medical Center." But that was not at all what my husband was talking about!

CHAPTER THREE

HEAVEN IS REAL!

By Ron

Though I was unaware of my shunt's failure to operate in this latest emergency I caused for my family and doctors, I do know that suddenly I stood at the gate of Heaven and knew exactly where I was! I was surrounded by a clear, bright but soft, transcendent light. Not like the sun, nor some man-made device, but a light beyond human experience.

At the entrance was a table with a massive book of parchment presided over by a heavenly person. I walked up to him and announced, "I'm ready to go in!" To my dismay, my name was not in the book. Seeing my determination to enter, the bookkeeper carefully turned the giant pages one by one, holding them with both hands and walking several steps to and fro. Just to appease me, he searched the columns again. My name was not there.

I couldn't believe it! In desperation I cried out, "Why? Why is my name not there? I've done all that is necessary to enter Heaven! I've accepted Jesus as my Lord and Savior. Have I been deceived?"

Hearing the commotion, another gentleman stepped out of Heaven and up to the table asking, "Can I be of service?" The keeper of the book explained my dilemma. This new man offered to go inside Heaven to double check. With renewed confidence, I expected my delay would soon be over.

More at ease now, I noticed a low hum of voices, sounding like an auditorium filled with people. Able to hear the hum but not able to distinguish any particular conversation, I asked, "What is all this noise?"

Apparently thinking my question odd, the bookkeeper returned, "Don't you know? These are all intercessory prayers coming up on your behalf!"

Taken aback, I blurted out, "You've got to be kidding!"

"No!" he answered, "would you like to hear one?"

"Sure," I said.

Immediately, I was actually taken to the exact place— my former church. Viewing the scene as if from the balcony, I watched my close friend, Mabry, at the pulpit praying. I was pleasantly surprised to see him on the platform, filling another role in the service as a break from his usual position in the sound booth. As he ended his prayer with, ". . . and restore this young man's health," I found myself back at the table at the entrance of Heaven, and the hum of the crowd resumed.

Although I appreciated and was deeply touched by this concern for me, I felt a bit quarrelsome. You see, I did not *want* their prayers answered. I *wanted* to enter Heaven! I yearned to fall and worship at Jesus' feet and undeservingly kiss the ground where He had just walked.

I now became aware of another sound. Taking a few steps to the left of the foyer table I heard more voices, distinctly children's voices. It sounded as if a host of little ones were playing in a babbling stream of water just on the other side of the barrier to Heaven. Though the wall appeared clear, I could not pass or even see through it, yet angels were passing back and forth freely. As I listened, one voice was raised above the others. Quickly I walked to the wall to get closer. Unmistakably, I knew! This was the voice of my son, Jason, who would have been three years old had he lived. Eager to go farther, I was restrained by a tall, masculine angel. He held his hand in front of my face and, with compelling authority, said, "That's far enough. Your son is fine, and he is well taken care of." Reluctantly I obeyed his command and walked back to the check-in table.

I became curious as to what was happening off to the right of the table. A new scene unfolded revealing a vast flow of humanity into Heaven. People of all ages including a multitude of quiet, orderly children were moving toward the source of the light.

The Lord was there welcoming each one as they came. Light radiated from and through Him. In my human experience and limited vocabulary, I cannot describe the magnificent beauty and stunning radiance of His countenance. Aware that I was watching, the Savior raised His arms to receive a particular young man who literally stood out above the crowd. At the point of embrace, Jesus made eye contact with me and spoke two words: "Remember this."

I was overwhelmed and honored beyond measure that He would speak to me! Yet I was puzzled at what He wanted me to "remember." Even so, the young man's face was forever stamped in my memory. He glanced at me and smiled as he neared the Master. Then he was engulfed in the flowing sleeves of Jesus' glowing white garment as he entered Heaven. Bewildered, I moved closer to look behind

Jesus. Then, suddenly, the reality of what I had seen dawned on me. He had passed *through* Jesus into Heaven! Heaven was on the other side and I was not to enter. Despite my disappointment, the truth of John 14:6 came alive to me: *"No one comes to the Father but through me."* (NASB). Could it be that the references to Jesus being the door and the gate into Heaven were not figurative as I had thought? My mind could scarcely contain what I had witnessed.

Years later, the Lord helped me to understand the wonder of what He had spoken. By the power of those two words, "Remember this!" He implanted details of the heavenly encounter so completely into my memory I would never forget, even though my physical memory would be severely impaired for years to come.

I will never forget Jesus' eyes! They were the focus of His entire being. His dark, blue, crystal clear eyes overflowed with a love that was beyond my comprehension. To see Him was to see love! Although He knew my heart and my thoughts, He accepted me as I was. I felt transformed in His sight, without faults or blemishes. *Love was in the form of a person!* I was keenly aware of His majesty: He was King of Kings and Lord of Lords. Yet, the relationship He imparted to me was Abba, Father—Daddy. I did not drop to my knees or fall on my face, as I had imagined, but felt accepted as part of *His family.*

Those wondrous eyes revealed yet another dimension: one of sadness. I could see reflected in his eyes another flow of people and a look of deep hurt for their refusal to accept His free gift of life and love. The power of His look spoke volumes of supernatural compassion.

The other man now returned from inside with a message. With sympathetic firmness he said, "It is not yet your time; your mission is not complete. You are being sent back, and I am going with you." With that, he escorted me back to the entrance table. It seems that my name was indeed in the Lamb's Book of Life. It simply was not time for me to leave the physical life; so my name was not in the first registry.

In an attempt to get them to reconsider, I foolishly demanded to see my wife. You see, at that time, I had no earthly memory of a wife. I had the silly notion that maybe an impossible request might allow entrance after all. In my scheme, I ruled God out; I seemed to think the conflict was simply between me and the angels. Sincerely, my heart's desire was to remain in the presence of my Savior and worship Him. Resorting to a bluff was my last hope to succeed.

At my demand, "I want to see my wife!" my escort nodded and said, "OK."

Immediately I was back in the operating room. The angel escort told me to get back inside my body. The surgical staff was working furiously to bring me back. One of the doctors had straddled my body and was literally pounding my chest in an effort to revive me. "That body . . . that body so full of pain and grief . . . you want me to get back in there?" At the angel's strong "Yes!" I had no choice but to slip back into my body, entering at the head.

Some time in recovery must have elapsed before I was coherent enough to focus in the natural realm. The angel had told me I would see my wife. He did not tell me how I would react. I had absolutely no memory of our life together, so as far as I was concerned, this was my first introduction to Glenda. Like Adam, who received Eve without knowing her history or even her personality, I was thrilled at my first sight of Glenda at my bedside. My spirit shouted, "Wow! Is this really the woman God has chosen for me?" I had just returned from Heaven where I had seen purity at its ultimate. He had saved the best, the refined for me. Like Adam, I was awed with the wife whom God had provided.

The angel who had escorted me from Heaven stayed to the right foot of my bed in the intensive care ward. I soon realized he was my guardian angel. What a constant source of encouragement and comfort he was. His smile was like no other. It truly was ear-to-ear, but it was also heavenly, full of the Father's love.

I tried to introduce him to everyone. My family just frowned and shook their heads. The nurses ignored my plea. Finally, in his kind voice, the angel convinced me, "Ron, they can neither see nor hear me. Just lie back and rest."

He was there to oversee my recovery, and, I think, to keep me from somehow sneaking back into Heaven. Just knowing he was there was strengthening and comforting. I found myself wanting to fall at his feet in worship. He solemnly rebuked me in a firm yet loving manner, saying, "We worship the same God."

The constant presence of the angel was such a consolation during those weeks in intensive care. On one occasion, the doctors blocked him from my view. In my struggle to see him, I noticed the doctors actually stepped back, clearing my view. No, they could not see him. Why did they step aside? I don't know, I only know I'm glad they did. The angel assured me, "Ron, I'm still here; just lie back and let the doctors do what they need to do. Relax."

Though the pressure in my head was diminishing, my optic nerve was under great stress. At times, I had no vision; at other times I could see clearly. An optical team brought in the "Big E" chart to check my sight. I could see it and beyond! In a mischievous mood, I read to them the tiny numbers on a metal surgical supply cart outside the room, through the open door. At that time, I must have had some residual effect of my heavenly body. One doctor in the group walked out into the hall to check what I had read. He had to rub his thumb across the print in order to read that line. Astounded, he came back and simply said, "Gentlemen, we don't need to check his eyes—put away the chart!"

During the weeks of recovery, I conversed with my angel. The first question was obvious: "What *is* my mission?"

He replied, "To win others to Christ and to strengthen other Christians." Then he added, "You can do this by sharing these experiences as your testimony."

I was not impressed, I thought this was the mission of every Christian, except for the special experience. I pursued other questions: "Since I am licensed to preach the gospel, is that my direction?"

"I cannot answer that for fear it would weaken your faith," he answered.

I asked about a business career and received the same response. It finally became apparent that I was not going to get the "inside scoop," so I gave up the issue.

Words cannot express other times of rich, rare conversation. But he always skillfully directed my remarks to praising the Lord. Our time together was spent in his teaching me to continually exalt the Lord and thank Him for every detail. It was a lesson in praying without ceasing. He was particularly diligent in keeping me focused on the Father and the infinite gift of His Son.

My angel had called me by name and said, "Ron, be slow in sharing your testimony."

"*Slow*!" I thought, "how can I be slow? I want to climb atop the highest building in Houston with a megaphone and shout '*Heaven is real! Put your life in order!*'"

Finally I was moved from intensive care to a private room for a few days of continued recovery before actually going home. On that day, the two surgeons who had become almost family to my loved ones, proudly approached my bed, patting each other on the back. They bragged about how great they were. "We were getting ready to send you to the morgue," they said, "but instead we're sending you home!"

I looked at my guardian angel. With his broad, loving smile, he said, "We know, don't we, Ron." He continued, "My mission is now complete, but please remember I'll always be around if you need me."

I glanced away for a second and when I looked back, he was gone. It was a bittersweet moment for me. From the early days of trying to introduce him to everyone to the priceless fellowship that I had enjoyed, I found being on my own to reestablish my relationship with my family a little intimidating. I felt I had lived a lifetime in those few weeks.

My health trials were in no way over, but the Lord had sent me back with one very major difference: I had encountered Jesus and had been commissioned to share!

CHAPTER FOUR

AMNESIA

By Ron

I 've heard it said that our need is our greatest security, because through it we are kept dependent upon God. This was truly the case during my nearly ten years of memory loss. My extraordinary need drew me like a magnet to the Lord. I couldn't remember what I had done ten minutes earlier, where I had parked, or even, at times, the names of my wife and children, but I never lost contact with my Lord.

"Praying without ceasing" became my way of life. Not constantly talking, but rather keeping the line of communication open. God was always with me, as demonstrated by the very real presence of my guardian angel, His special messenger.

One day, while running errands for Glenda, I drove to the post office without our oldest child, Jennifer, my usual errand companion. I suddenly found myself off the beaten path. Nothing looked familiar. In panic, I cried out, "Where am I? Which way do I turn?"

Leaning forward from the back seat in a rare moment of visibility, my angel simply pointed and said, "Turn here, Ron."

Relief flooded my soul! I sighed, "Thank you, Lord!" The Lord knew my need and He met it!

During these years of amnesia, and in an effort to retain my sanity, I did occasional part-time work. Once by word of mouth, we learned that an office supply house needed a delivery driver, a position normally held by eighteen-year-olds. As I applied for the job, I stretched the truth by telling the manager, "I am semi-retired and need work to fill my time." In fact, the extra income was needed just as much as the satisfaction of working. Also fearful of rejection, I carefully withheld information about my medical problems.

Assuming the driving route would be confined to the local area, I grew concerned when I learned I had to drive all over Houston. With God's help and using key maps, I managed to find the many locations. Once, the street I needed was not shown on the map. As I neared the general area I reduced my speed and somehow pulled right up to the business as if I knew where I was going all along. I whistled praise songs all the way back.

Occasionally there were days that my head hurt more than usual. But my employer did not call on those days, so I never had to turn him down. My job performance never alerted him to my physical disability. God was my portion, He filled the gap where my abilities lacked. The boss was pleased with my efficiency. This meant fewer hours and less expense for him and personal accomplishment for me. However, the manager eventually became wary of my intent and fearing I might contend for his job, he dismissed me.

The next year I delivered for another business, similar to the first, and all went well until Christmas time. My new employer asked me to deliver a van load of long, rectangular-shaped boxes. These were gifts to all his clients and suppliers. On the third stop, one box was opened in front of me. It was whiskey! I was delivering whiskey! Feeling absolutely sick and naive, I drove back to the shop to resign my job. My own struggle with alcohol years earlier would not let me put this potential poison into others' hands. I told the owner, "I'm a Christian and I just can't deliver these gifts. I'm so sorry." My heart was heavy with dread as I drove home. I had just forfeited the Christmas money we had hoped to have. Glenda readily supported me and upheld the integrity of my decision.

Two days later the owner called—what a surprise! "Ron, could you deliver something else?"

Could I? Yes! I rushed over to find his back room stacked with smaller, flat boxes with a freshly printed greeting for each one. Chocolates! He had replaced the liquor with candy! I loaded the van and took off. Several recipients called the owner immediately to thank him. This was the most thoughtful gift their office had ever received since the boxes were opened on the spot and shared with the employees, rather than being taken home by the boss. After the holidays, I wasn't called back. But that was OK. God was still in control!

As an early retiree, my dad had helped my mother with the housework and the meals. He had been a baker on a ship in World War II, and continued to bake bread at home as a hobby. He became my role model of what a husband-at-home should be. Never fearing a loss of masculinity, I took over the heavier housework and many of the routine errands.

I bought a bread making book and began baking. The upside-down pecan rolls, buttery almond bear claws and the croissants communicated love to my family and helped me cope with my constant headache. As long as I concentrated on a recipe, the more complex the better, I didn't seem to notice the pain. I experimented with everything in the book. The aromas of English crumpets, German streuselkuchen or French sourdough bread filled our house almost daily. My low-cost hobby served my family, won acclaim from my dad and gave me a focus.

The old cliché, "Necessity is the mother of invention" became true for me. I found creative ways to compensate for my lack of memory. As I worked, I would line the counter with all the ingredients I measured out, in the order they were to be used, then put them back into the cabinet after they were added to the recipe. If distracted for even a second, I could forget my last step if the system was not in place. God blessed my efforts with confidence to tackle more complicated recipes with success. I praised Him continually!

When Jennifer was in second grade, my sister introduced me to burritos. Any fan of Mexican food knows how good they are! I learned to cook four pounds of pinto beans overnight and spend most of the next day rolling the tortillas with beans and cheese. I then individually wrapped and packed them for the freezer. It was Jennifer's favorite lunch that school year. My family and friends eventually convinced me to sell the burritos as a home industry. For one year the burrito money helped meet our bills. After loading a fresh batch into the freezer, we often joked, "If they don't sell, we can always *eat* the inventory." The order for a few dozen always coincided with an expense that was currently due. God was always on time!

To keep my life functioning, Glenda and I devised little memory systems. For instance, the orange juice was kept in an orange plastic pitcher. Glenda sewed a bag with tiny pockets to store my insulin vials and needles to keep track of my two daily shots. The insulin shots were so routine that remembering them was quite a challenge. Now, anyone could look at the bag to tell if I'd had my shot.

The simplest tasks were not to be taken for granted. I needed a routine for showering that could not be interrupted. Otherwise I would step out of the shower with shampoo still in my hair!

During my years with Sears, I developed the habit of carrying a note pad in my hip pocket. Now, the little pad was vital. Everywhere I went, I wrote down the make and model of the car I was in and where it was parked. I jotted down the names of people I met, so I could share them with Glenda. I left nothing to chance—everything was recorded on that little pad.

Of course, I posted the master list in the car, where I was going, in the order of the stops. Glenda drew me large, simple maps. I sensed I was not alone. God was with me, directing, literally, my every step. He was part of me!

Details of my disability puzzled even me. I could read, write, spell, drive, even work mathematical problems. Oddly, I recalled remote, trivial details from my childhood. From a television series in the late '50s and early '60s, I remembered that "Songbird" was the name of the airplane on *Sky King,* that Roy Rogers's dog was named "Bullet," and that "Nellie Belle" was the name of Pat Brady's jeep. I impressed my friends and enjoyed the comic relief that these conversations produced.

My doctor said, "Ron, your memory is shot, but your judgment is very good." He encouraged me more than he knew, by telling me my decision-making processes were still intact.

But it was the Lord who really kept me going. My only reliable area of memory was in spiritually related matters. I could sing hymns, quote and recognize scripture and discuss sermons and topics pertaining to church. *And* I remembered every detail of my Heaven Experience! On the night that I lay awake in bed and told Glenda the story, I feared I might lose it soon. The next morning I said, "Write down everything I tell you—I'm afraid I may forget something." I'm so happy to report that I never even read the notes; every detail has remained vividly clear.

We called our pastor for an appointment. "We need to tell you what I experienced while I was in the hospital." After we told him, we asked, "Can this be real?"

"Yes," he answered, "it certainly is. And I have advice for you: First, you will have opportunities to share this story; as you do, give God the glory for it. Next, your memory being what it is, you shouldn't read any books or other accounts on near-death experiences. You don't want to accidentally exchange details or become confused." This was excellent counsel.

I wanted to tell everyone I saw what had happened to me. Glenda sensed my impulsiveness and began to warn me, "Honey, be careful whom you tell. Don't be grabbing people off the street!"

"OK," I agreed, "I'll try to contain my enthusiasm." But I still had the most wonderful sense of purpose to share my testimony. People were intrigued and willing to hear . . . until one day, when a neighbor was helping me with a plumbing emergency. I began to share with him—I wanted to give him something of value in exchange for his services. I began by telling him about my guardian angel. He interrupted and began arguing. Glenda heard loud voices coming from the bedroom.

"What was *that* all about?" she asked me when we were alone.

Upon reflection, I had to admit that in this case my motivation for sharing my most precious possession, my testimony, was out of a sense of duty, almost an obligation. I felt the sting of my disobedience when I did not have godly discernment. The problem was with me, not my neighbor. I suddenly understood my guardian angel's counsel to be *slow*.

I repented and vowed that day, "Lord, I'll always ask for Your wisdom and know that You are leading me to share from now on."

I told my testimony many times during the years of amnesia. Originally sharing with individuals, I eventually had invitations to speak to small groups and I was concerned over how I could handle discerning God's will. But soon the Lord put my mind at rest: He showed me that He was in charge of sending whomever He wanted. I just smiled when someone would say, "I've invited several to the service tonight and I can't explain why they're not here." The number in a group never mattered to me. One or one hundred—the Holy Spirit's presence was all that counted.

In spite of this, at times during the ten long years I almost broke under the health battle. My headaches were severe and almost unbearable. My mental condition was devastating. Depression awaited me any time I focused on my physical limitations. At times I was so frustrated over the severe pain, I felt I could not go on another minute. I wished God would take me back to Heaven. In anguish I would declare, "Glenda, I can't take it anymore. My head is killing me and my memory is worse than ever." Each time she would stop whatever she was doing and pray with me, crying out to God for help and wisdom.

She consoled me, "Honey, your mission is not over. Let God decide when you are to come *home*." Glenda's reminder and God's mercy and overwhelming love would always encourage me to keep on keeping on.

Saturday, May 16, 1992 was one of those days. I awoke

with intense pain and even less memory than usual. Not able to call my wife's name, I asked her for her purse. I secretly opened her billfold to read her name from her driver's license. (How I knew to do this I'm not sure.) The Bible church we had joined had scheduled an afternoon fellowship at a member's home for a fish-fry. We had not planned to attend. However, in an effort to get my mind off my headache Glenda urged, "Let's go to the fellowship, it'll be fun for all of us."

As I tried to cope with the pain, I finally relented, "All right, get good directions." As we were driving the 20 miles to the cookout, a rainstorm struck with such intensity that visibility was virtually zero. It was all I could do to keep from turning back.

Then we drove out of the rain and realized the ground was dry in the direction we were headed. As we pulled into the parking area, we saw tables set up on the back lawn. Church members were gathering and playing dominoes while the host and others fried the catfish. I had to force myself to be civil. Glenda prompted me with several friends' names as we mingled with the crowd. The strategy for survival was to involve myself in the group and to focus away from the pain. But this time, I was losing.

After two miserable hours of not-so-successful coping, the time came to eat. I was not in the least hungry. My blood sugar was too high. Aware that I had taken my insulin, Glenda shoved a plate in my hands and flatly insisted, "You must find something to eat." (For a diabetic, church buffets are often forbidden fruit.) This was one more challenge I didn't think I could handle.

People were already drifting back to the serving table for second helpings as I passed up all the salads and put a couple of pieces of catfish on my plate. Just one or two hush puppies and some coffee to drink was more than enough.

Then my eyes fell on a large white turkey platter holding one small fried flounder. (I later learned it was there as a joke for someone who liked flounder—not catfish.) As I saw the lone fish, mental images of being with friends in an air boat on the bay suddenly flashed through my mind. I could see their faces and remember their names. "That's a flounder," I said, "I've been *floundering*!"

At the same moment I felt a sensation in my head. God took my headache away and poured the memory in! "Glenda, it's back! It's all back!" Standing across the counter from me, she instantly knew what I meant.

"Ed King . . . Chuck Brummet . . . Earl Butler . . . ," I began to name friends on the coast with whom I'd gone fishing. My church buddies had taken me out only a couple of times in their flat bottomed boat, in shallow water, with a spotlight to gig flounder . . . fifteen years earlier! And now I could remember each man! Although we had enjoyed the fish, I hadn't particularly enjoyed missing a night's sleep to stay out fishing in the cold, salty, damp air. But I could recall the entire experience!

"Do you remember our first meeting? . . . our wedding? . . . the births of our children?" Glenda urgently asked.

"Yes! Yes! I remember it all! Oh, Praise the Lord!" I exclaimed.

In total awe, I didn't want to move, yet I wanted to leap and shout! Glenda and I joined the group out on the lawn. We confided in our closest friends. They began to pass the news along and soon the miracle monopolized the conversation of the entire party.

These good-hearted people had known us for less than a year. I had camouflaged my poor memory and had hidden the severity of my headaches from them. So, they hadn't a clue as to the magnitude of what had just happened to me. Many smiled and expressed genuine joy in our good fortune as they continued to enjoy the meal.

Glenda and I could not eat. With our hearts pounding, we excused ourselves. Where could we go? We walked over to our parked car. With this much privacy we stood trembling, tears flowing. All we could do was praise God. "I can't believe it, but it's true. Praise you, Father!" "Hallelujah! Thank you, thank you, Lord!" We were speechless, but not silent!

Unlike the caution my guardian angel had given me in sharing about Heaven, I boldly told everyone my memory was back. Grocery clerks, postal workers, car mechanics—anyone with whom I had contact I cornered to tell them my news. Without restraints, I proclaimed, "For ten years I had no memory, but God has restored it! Now it's all back!"

THE LUFKIN DAILY NEWS

Religion

Saturday, November 19, 1994

Woodlawn Baptist

Mt. Pleasant Missionary Baptist

TOTAL RECALL

Lufkinite regains memory after coping with brain injury for 10 years

By BRONWYN TURNER
Staff Writer

700 Club films local man's story

☐ 'Miracle' gets national attention

By JIM JOHNSTON

Lufkinite Shares Testimony

Life Light

STAFF WRITER
Wanda Pridgen

"Remember this!" was the only thing Ron Pettey of Lufkin COULD remember during his decade-long period of amnesia.

That message came to Ron from Christ as h

Jesus and became owner of some information that would only be confirmed and totally documented, by physical evidence, 10 years later, after his memory returned.

He also

By the end of summer, news of the miracle reached the local newspaper. A Christian reporter captured the heartbeat of our joy in an article that appeared on the front page of the Sunday paper. With this publicity came invitations to speak in churches. Thus, God opened the door for His testimony to be heard by hundreds more.

The snowball effect continued. Two years later, the "700 Club" nationally aired the re-enactment of my memory loss and its miraculous return. The local Christian radio and TV stations then asked us to share the whole story of my Heaven experience. Glenda and I were later interviewed on a TBN affiliate station. In the program's closing moments, the host asked, "Ron, if you had just one minute left to say anything to anyone in the world, what would it be?"

That was easy to answer. I said, "Believe in the Lord Jesus Christ and you shall be saved. Heaven is real—It is not a fairyland or a make-believe place, it is real! . . . And there's only one way to get there: believe in the Lord Jesus Christ. Jesus is where life begins and ends, He is the Alpha and the Omega."

"Cable television—God's *megaphone!*" Glenda exclaimed on the drive home that day. God revealed to us that He was fulfilling my heart's desire. The ridiculous expression I voiced years earlier about climbing atop the highest building to gain an audience had actually become reality. God was honoring the aspiration He had placed in my heart by using technology that He created to accomplish His will.

CHAPTER FIVE

THE WIFE'S PERSPECTIVE

By Glenda

I took a monumental step in my personal walk with God when I released Ron into His care on Saturday night before the traumatic surgery. My salvation experience as an adolescent had always been sure. Now, at age thirty-one, I began to place all my expectations, hope and emotions—everything that I was—into God's hands. I had already shifted my allegiance from my parents to my husband at the time of our marriage. Now, I transferred everything to the spiritual realm, and felt safe in *"the shadow of His wings"* (Psalm 36:7).

God told me that night He was giving Ron back, that he would be OK. When the surgery was finished the next day, I had supernatural peace that only God can give. My fear of widowhood was gone. I trusted God with my life, my children and the future. My concern for material possessions and physical abilities faded in His sufficiency.

Ron's physical recovery was a slow process of rebuilding for a body that had become thin and fragile. His shaved head was tender with scars. However, even then God gave me an optimistic spirit. I didn't see Ron as he was. I saw the husband God had returned to me—kind and loving, sensitive and protective. His personality had not changed. He was the same witty, generous and caring gentleman I had married.

God certainly got my attention through the trauma. The more time I spent in prayer, the closer Ron and I became. More alert to his needs, I was in a state of constant intercessory prayer for my husband.

Although I never doubted Ron's testimony of Heaven, the Holy Spirit confirmed the truth of it in the months and years to follow.

As soon as Ron was physically able, we drove to Port Lavaca to visit with our longtime friends, Jean and Mabry Cain. (God had created a special niche in Ron's heavenly memory for this couple.) They were astounded that we would make the trip so soon in Ron's recovery. Did we have something to share! Ron, with eyes dancing, couldn't wait to tell Mabry, "I heard you pray for me in church and I know what you said!"

With a bewildered expression, Mabry agreed, "Yes, Ron, we prayed for you many times."

Filling Mabry in on the entire testimony helped him understand that Ron was talking about a specific prayer. After remembering that the services had been recorded, he and Ron went to the church to search out the tape. Without hesitation, Ron repeated the phrase he had heard, ". . . and restore this young man's health." As the tape was played there was a visible reaction in Mabry! It was undeniable proof, Ron had miraculously witnessed our friend's prayer!

One day in January Ron shared the miracle in three separate sessions, two with individuals and one with a group of men. God was exalted and gloriously praised all three times. The next day, however, Ron hit bottom emotionally. His detached, lethargic expression was a complete contrast to the day before. I was frightened! This drastic mood swing had never happened before.

"I'm fine," he repeatedly claimed as I questioned him. Previous experience with Ron told me there was nothing medically wrong, even though his pale, forlorn countenance suggested otherwise. By late afternoon, he finally admitted to me that he felt like he was *dying*. I immediately dropped everything and prayed aloud, at his side.

Through my tears, with wavering voice, I cried out to God, "Lord, the guardian angel said he'd be around if Ron needed him. Well, Father, if the angel could help, I ask you to let him be here now!"

ZAP! There was an immediate change in the room's atmosphere. With my own eyes, I saw the gloom lift and color return to Ron's face! Instantly he was laughing and crying! "What happened? What did you see or hear?" my voice quivered.

Catching his breath he said, "I heard my angel speak—*Not yet, Ron!*"

Just as we had conferred with our pastor over Ron's out-of-body experience, we were back in his office for counsel again. He helped us understand that a spiritual war was raging. Satan was losing ground so he had to fight back the only way he could, by attacking a weakness. Satan had tried to convince Ron that it was time to go back where he really wanted to be, to leave the earth. But, God was victorious! Gloriously, I witnessed God's intervening with the angel's presence. *All at once, the entire testimony was unconditionally validated for me!*

Throughout Ron's survival and recovery, I continued to lean on the Lord instead of my husband. I enjoyed freedom to love, help and serve Ron while I daily found that Jehovah

Jireh (God's attribute of being our provider) confirmed His nature to me. Ron never worried about finances or the future and eventually I, too, began to relax. Laying the details of daily life at Jesus' feet relieved me of carrying the heavy responsibility.

However, like Ron, when I took my eyes off Jesus, I too began to sink. Satan took full advantage of the darkness of night. Anxiety would overtake me. More than a few times I cried myself to sleep. Imagining the worst-case scenario of *what if* Ron never improved and I had a nervous breakdown was certainly not of the Lord. However, in the morning, I couldn't even muster up these fearful thoughts. Spiritually, light and dark don't mix. It was clearly the enemy.

A spiritual breakthrough came in 1985. On the first Sunday evening of that year our pastor flipped the pages of his Bible to Joel 2:25 and read God's promise, " . . . *I will restore to you the years that the locusts have eaten . . .*" He went on to explain the meaning and implications of that passage. The verse pierced my heart. For the first time in my life, a scripture seemed to be just for me.

With my parents baby-sitting, Ron and I were alone on the drive home. My tears poured like rain during the entire twenty-minute drive. I was claiming that message for us! This *rhema* from God gave me hope. I examined all we had lost: Ron's health, his memory *and* our son Jason, stillborn in 1979! I sensed God had put the ball in my court. Would I trust Him to restore a son to our family? For many days, I privately pondered this. So much in my life was at stake. Yes! I would trust God!

Before the year was out, we heard my obstetrician exclaim, "It's a boy!" in the delivery room. God had given us Douglas, the first phase of restoration.

Many have asked how I handled the ten years of memory loss. In a nutshell my answer is "Grace, God's grace!"

As circumstances revealed the severity of my husband's disability, God, in His mercy and grace, carried me through.

Things normal people took for granted threw Ron a curve. For example, once, before sitting for a family portrait, I had my hair cut and styled at the beauty shop. When I returned home, Ron could not conceal his bewilderment. He did not recognize me! Naive as to the depth of Ron's confusion, I pushed the incident aside but vowed this would never happen again.

My heart broke to learn that close relationships for Ron would fade in as little as two weeks if there was no interaction. The first time a dear friend moved away was a somber experience, as Ron had to be reintroduced the next time they met. From week to week he had to be reminded of names of our church friends. He didn't seem to forget the routine or the significance of attending church, just the names and backgrounds of people.

My rhema, God's revelation, became a source of faith and promise. His word kept me sane as I dealt daily with the state of our lives. I had to concentrate on the fact that God had spared Ron's life, allowed him a glimpse of Heaven, and even now, was affirming him in sharing the testimony. The greatest blessing was that Ron's love for the Lord and lost humanity shown with a passion. We were living examples of what Paul wrote in II Corinthians 12:10, ". . . *For when I am weak, then I am strong.*" Jesus had taught, "*My grace is sufficient for thee: for my strength is made perfect in weakness*" (verse 9). God humbled us as we knew that He uses the simple things to confound the wise.

In retrospect, I realize that God shielded me from the full knowledge of Ron's inability to remember. He even controlled my curiosity. Several times I should have pursued a matter, but just dropped it. The Lord further held Ron back from telling me all his thoughts when he was confused. God protected me from the truth that would have been devastating at the time. He knew my frailty. I can take no credit for having strength of my own.

The Lord gave me an optimistic and creative spirit. Sewing became my hobby and outlet for expression. God's hands were in my projects—plaids and stripes *accidentally* matched, leftover scraps fit just where I needed them. The personal satisfaction I gained from dressing the girls and making accessories for the home outweighed the economics.

Like clay in the potter's hands, I became pliable. God's plans were agreeable as He communicated them through Ron. I grew content in my position of being submissive. With sound biblical teaching coming through our pastor, I saw Ron as God's provision for me—my protection, spiritually and physically. God showed me over and over that as I would trust Him, *He* would provide our every need. I accepted the fact that Ron could not work. Jeopardizing his health with a job independent of God's plan would be disastrous. Times of employment would come as God brought them to us. I could remain a mother-at-home where I was needed.

When Christian school tuition payments became too challenging to meet, Ron suggested we teach the children at home. My first thoughts of home-educating did not set well. Just the idea was outrageous and preposterous. I feared isolation and cringed at the sacrifice of my time. I furiously resisted the conviction God had given Ron. However, like working the clay, God softened my heart. He sent a seasoned home-schooling family into our neighborhood and church, and they led us to the area support group. Ron and I both were amazed at the large number of families involved. Mingling with like-minded Christians, we were blessed with academic help, activities, field trips and social outings. By the end of the first year, the change in our oldest daughter was dramatic. Jennifer had grown to accept and love her toddler sister and had developed a bold, new self-confidence. I knew God had cultivated patience in me that I had not had before, along with an unselfish desire to work with the children. I now whole-heartedly shared Ron's commitment.

With in-depth teaching from the Old Testament on family, the Lord urged Ron to sell our house and return to his hometown. Again I resisted. Although no career was holding us, leaving our church and familiar surroundings seemed risky. Besides, I loved our home. After a series of mishaps, a hurricane and a leaking hot water heater, God had given us a beautiful wooden deck and new carpet throughout. We were just beginning to enjoy these improvements when I found myself back on the potter's wheel where God gently changed my heart again. We signed a realtor's contract and about two weeks later learned the wonderful news that I was expecting our fourth child! This was a new test of faith. "Had we missed God's timing for the move?" I wondered.

With only a few days left on the contract, a buyer came forth. We sold the house and moved into a rental home in Lufkin, Texas, one month before the baby arrived.

In this obviously difficult time, God was most gracious to me. On my last check-up in Houston, the doctor said the baby was not turning and settling into the birth position on time. I was preparing myself for a Cesarean delivery. However, in Lufkin, we consulted midwives. Three weeks before Kelli's birth the midwives came to our house, carefully examined my condition and safely turned Kelli around to the proper position. The love of God overwhelmed me! I was spared the pain of surgery and the great financial burden that it would have placed upon us. Our new daughter was perfectly healthy and my recovery, at age thirty-eight, was the easiest of the four births.

God blessed us mightily as we obeyed his command to honor Ron's parents, a first step in restoring the family. Our children have cherished the time spent with grandparents. Fishing on the lake, the fascination of gardening and grandmother's wonderful home cooking are just a few of the many rewards. The benefits were mutual. Holding a two-hour-old granddaughter and being an integral part of that new life was priceless for them. More than once, the children's visits and cheery homemade cards to an ailing grandparent demonstrated the truth of Proverbs 17:22, *"A merry heart doeth good like a medicine . . ."*

As I meditate on these and other blessings, I continue to be overwhelmed with unspeakable joy over the gift of our two younger children. Who could imagine having children in the condition Ron was in? Had we listened to well-meaning family and friends, these precious children would not be here today. I praise the Lord for aligning us with pastors and teachers who taught that children are indeed a blessing from God and for the Holy Spirit for confirming this truth to us. Our children are growing up in a climate experiencing His presence. They understand that only through the Lord do we *". . . live and move and have our being!"* (Acts 17:28).

"Grandchildren are the crown of old men, and the glory of sons is their fathers"—Proverbs 17:6 (NASB)

CHAPTER SIX

TINY MEMBERS

By Ron

We have previously written of the *sea* of people flowing into Heaven. A vast multitude of children were part of this sea. The smaller children were being led or carried by adults and older children. As they approached the Lord, whoever had a hand free, whether child or adult, had his hands held out, and each hand was enveloped in a cloud-like vapor. I wondered what the children were carrying as I stared into the misty coverings. As I looked, the vapor rolled off and I saw a miniature human in each hand, fully mature, clothed, uniquely beautiful and complete. I felt numb as I realized what I was seeing! Each the size of a finger, these tiny adults were babies miscarried or aborted from their mothers' wombs shortly after God gave them life. I somehow knew that they were carried not because they were undeveloped or could not walk, but to show the great love of the Father for them.

"Shalom." Jesus received each child. On a divine schedule, Jesus separately greeted each one, calling *everyone* by his new, heavenly name. The Lord's warm, personal welcome demonstrated His full knowledge of every individual—each life as well as his time of arrival. A gleeful, home-coming joy shown on each child's face.

Meditating on this scene makes the scriptures come alive!

"*. . . Thou hast covered me in my mother's womb. . . . I am fearfully and wonderfully made. . . . Thine eyes did see my substance, yet being unperfect; and in thy book all my members were written . . . when as yet there was none of them. How precious also are thy thoughts unto me, O God! How great is the sum of them!*" (Psalm 139:13, 14, 16, 17).

Jesus tells us in Matthew 18:5-6 the consequences of our disregard for children: "*. . . Whoso shall receive one such little child in My name receiveth Me. But whoso shall offend (hurt) one of these little ones which believe in Me, it were better for him that a millstone were hanged about his neck, and that he were drowned in the depth of the sea.*"

These scriptures and the adult status of these marvelous individuals forever settle for me the argument as to whether these aborted people are fetal tissue or human beings. Through the eyes of God they are viewed as wondrous demonstrations of His creative power. From the beginning of time, before the moment of conception, God sees what each of us will become in every lifestyle and occupation, whether living for or against the Creator. In His infinite knowledge He knows the duration of each life. Through His incredible mercy the Lord brings these young ones into fellowship with Himself. All are endowed by the Master with individual talents and abilities; they experience the full scope of His love.

The magnitude of the love of God for these tiny members of His kingdom is truly beyond mortal understanding. In ways too awesome to grasp, Jesus loves *all* the children of the world in His own special way, including those not allowed the privilege to live. I am speechless reflecting upon the miracle that God allowed me to experience: looking beyond time and space, perceiving the future stature of an infantile life, seeing for a moment through Jesus' eyes. In His presence *agape* love prevailed. I sensed how each child was absolutely precious, uniquely significant and completely cared for.

I can understand these truths only by God's spirit. The Lord's gift of this vision and discernment is a manifestation of His grace, completely unmerited and undeserved by anything I have done. Jesus commanded me to "Remember" and to share what I experienced. All the Glory is His!

CHAPTER SEVEN

SCOTTY!

By Ron

In February, 1993, Glenda and I were enjoying a Bible Study group that met on Thursday nights in the home of a friend. This twelve-week session was being led by a pharmacist from a town an hour away. We were working through a book entitled *Experiencing God*. Little did we know with what magnitude the title would become reality.

As the weeks progressed, the leader shared prayer needs from his home church. Most urgent was a request to pray for a young man suffering from a failed kidney transplant. We were gripped by the account of this family's struggle.

Carolyn Hennigan had grown weary making the long trips to the hospital with her son, Scotty, for dialysis treatments. Now, as his body rejected the medications with allergic reactions, Carolyn wept before the Lord. Remembering the very words Jesus had spoken, she uttered them herself: "Let this cup pass from me, but nevertheless, let thy will be done." On one of her next excursions to the hospital, she lovingly squeezed Scotty's knee and told him, "I'm ready for you to be healed, *whatever* that takes!" With a smile, Scotty agreed.

As the two came home that evening the house was especially quiet. The phone did not ring, the doorbell was silent, even the dogs were hushed. The Lord had put a "holy seal" over their house. The Comforter was with Carolyn as she checked on Scotty during the night and found that while he slept peacefully, he had gone *home*.

Carolyn wanted to meet with our prayer group to share God's working in her life. Just three weeks after the funeral, she was ready to share how her stress and grief had turned to joy as only the presence of the Lord could bring. She attributed her radiant smile and quiet acceptance of God's plan to what she described as "the Lord's protective bubble" over her.

Later, the Bible study over, and for no reason at all, I asked Carolyn if she had a picture of Scotty with her. Startled, she explained, "It's strange you should ask me that!" She carefully removed a framed picture from a large handbag. "As I was going out the door this evening, I felt compelled to go back inside to get this picture. I had to bring it!"

Chill bumps raised on my arms. The young man I had seen the Lord embrace and welcome into Heaven eleven years earlier now had a name: he was Scotty! Scotty had gazed at me with an expression of absolute satisfaction as he neared Jesus. I had gotten a good look at the twenty-one-year-old. Scotty's face was keenly imprinted on my memory.

On my knees now, I stammered, "That was Scotty! I have no doubt! But *how* could I have seen him eleven years in advance?"

The others in the group that night rallied around Carolyn and me, reminding us that Heaven is not bound by our earthly limits of time. One hymnist wrote, "When the trumpet of the Lord shall sound, and *time* shall be no more ..." which is supported by scripture (Revelation 21:1, 22:5). In the New Testament we read, "... *One day is with the Lord as a thousand years, and a thousand years as one day.*" 2 Peter 3:8. We had to take hold of these truths by faith because we lacked understanding.

Carolyn was moved as I shared what I had clearly seen that day so long ago. Jesus had welcomed her son with open arms as He looked over to me and said, "Remember this!" That He could, and would, look ahead in time to comfort a grieving mother. What love! How incredibly wise and compassionate!

God isn't limited by the earth's time frame. He sees the whole picture at once. He operates in His own way and His own time to accomplish His good and perfect will in us. The Creator carefully weaves and works the elements of our lives, like an intricate tapestry, into something pleasing to Him. The pain and grief of losing a loved one is never beautiful to those who suffer, but God alone is able to work all things to the best for those who trust Him (the message of Romans 8:28).

His loving care that day at Heaven's gate touched us in many ways. He comforted a grieving mother. He became an anchor and foundation for the years of my amnesia. My memory of these blessed events remained sparkling clear, even when I couldn't remember my family. The Savior had said, "Remember this!" With a striking clarity I remember, and even *I* am astounded.

CHAPTER EIGHT

GOD OUR PROVIDER

By Ron

God has guided our lives in spite of our shortcomings. In His infinite mercy, the Lord redeemed us from our own blunders, showing us that His ways are higher than ours. He was incredibly patient with us while we were (and are) so slow to learn. May our testimony encourage you to take charge over areas of your life through the truth of His word and the power of His spirit.

The list of financial blessings could fill a book of their own! Before God got our attention we were always struggling financially. During the late '70s when we were active in running our home business, we foolishly made 90-day bank loans as a merchandising strategy. This created a never-ending cycle of stress. Only God's intervention broke the cycle.

Expensive car repairs were a given. Then, a few years of paying private school tuition tested our commitment to tithe.

We had never debated giving God the first ten percent of our income. We had even settled the question whether to tithe on the net or the gross of our paychecks early in our marriage. But during the mid '80s, with income dwindling and bills mounting, the checks to the church had simply not been written.

At the peak of this crisis, our pastor invited a CPA from the West Coast to hold a weekend seminar on finances. For the first time, Glenda and I understood that giving God the first ten percent was symbolic of acknowledging that it all belonged to Him. If any good was to come out of the remaining ninety percent, it would be only by His divine power to protect and stretch it!

Malachi 3:10-11 shouted a message for us. *"Bring ye all the tithes into the storehouse, that there may be meat in mine house, and* prove me *now herewith, saith the Lord of hosts, if I will not open the windows of* Heaven, *and pour you out a blessing that there shall not be room enough to receive it . . . And I will* rebuke the devourer *for your sakes, and he shall not destroy the fruits of your ground . . ."*

On paper, the numbers seemed impossible. My wife and I repented of getting ahead of the Lord by borrowing. The loans only showed our impatience to have what we wanted with an attitude of independence. Without sharing our financial status with anyone, we began tithing with a new depth of conviction. We evaluated each decision from a fresh perspective and asked God for help. Deleting the school tuition payments was obvious. Eating out was forbidden. Careful grocery shopping and calculated use of fuel in the car were always considered. Could we trust God to sustain our family without health insurance? Yes, we would. We were partners in a new relationship with the Master of the universe. He would not disappoint us!

The ultimate lesson the Lord was teaching us was

to be content with His sovereign plans. We heard some encouraging advice: "God isn't as concerned with where you are as much as with the direction in which you are moving."

Our first test of contentment came soon after we agreed to cut up the credit cards. The refrigerator went out! Normally we would have considered this a necessity and made an exception to our agreement. But instead we recognized the opportunity God was giving us to wait on Him. We brought in the Igloo, froze a block of ice in our chest freezer, and pared down to milk and orange juice. We called a repair man to assess the damage. On faith, we told him, "As soon as we have the $350 to replace the compressor, we'll call you." He was so stunned when we did not order the part that he forgot to charge us for the service call. We needed the Igloo for just a few days because a family from church learned of our need and gave us a refrigerator they had sitting in a vacant house. God had rebuked the devourer, just as He said He would! We were blessed and our faith took a giant leap forward!

It seemed that the more we submitted our wills to God, the more He responded with blessings. A couple of years earlier, my parents had generously given us a Chevrolet Suburban, but now they suddenly insisted on underwriting the repairs. We felt as if we had been given a raise!

We knew we were moving in the right direction when some time later, my parents sent us a $100 check in the mail and we did not have an immediate need for it. Imagine that! We offered to return it, but they refused. At their suggestion, we kept it in a desk drawer. About a week later, a rock shattered the back window on our Suburban. We dreaded the expense of getting it fixed. During my morning shower the next day I suddenly *knew* what the cost would be . . . $100! God was teaching us to trust Him! Sure enough, the auto-glass shop estimate was $100. When

I picked up my vehicle, the ticket read $99.75!

"Go buy yourself a Coke," the owner joked as he handed me the quarter change. God had a sense of humor! Walking with Him became exciting! (We are now enjoying our third Suburban and second car as gifts from my parents.)

During the summer of 1986, God led us into homeschooling. A year later we began to catch on to His larger scope of reuniting and blessing the family. Academics were elementary. I found my heart and thoughts turning to my wife and children. Our days began with reading Psalms and Proverbs and praying. We read often that *"wisdom is the principal thing"* and that God wanted us to ask for it and treasure it (Proverbs 4:7).

Soon our concern turned to Glenda's mother. Twice widowed, Helyn lived a full eight hours away. Our hearts' desire was for her to share our convictions of family so she could move closer and enjoy a warm relationship with her only grandchildren. We hoped our move to Lufkin in 1989 would encourage her to join us. Others agreed with us in prayer. However, our optimism was always followed by disappointments. Her upscale retirement patio home and complex with all the planned activities seemed no match for a rental duplex in East Texas. We were stunned in May of 1993 when Helyn phoned. With a lilt in her voice, she said, "Are you sitting down? I have news for you—I'm ready to come to Lufkin."

Our jaws dropped. "What changed your mind?" I asked.

"The *Lord* did," she replied without hesitation, "and all my friends are encouraging me."

"Friends?" I thought. "The same ones who only weeks ago warned her to the contrary?—God has done a great work!"

With courage from above, we had the joy of helping Helyn relocate in July. Her new focus and attitude of contentment seemed too good to be true. She busied herself in making new friends and learning her way around town. It was obvious that the Lord was in control.

As the months unfolded, God honored my dear mother-in-law beyond anyone's expectations. She met Bill, a wonderful Christian widower whose banjo strumming matched her piano genius. With a toe-tapping repertoire of ragtime, bluegrass and gospel music, they were a match for each other! The following spring I was honored to perform my first official ministerial business of marrying the pair.

But the happy ending does not stop there. One year later our town was suddenly drenched with four inches of rain in the early morning hours. Most of the town was flooded, including both of our homes. What seemed to be a disaster turned into a blessing. After the clean-up, Bill decided to move his bride to higher ground. They bought a lovely newer home and offered us their home at a family price! We rejoiced! After six years of renting with no down payment saved, we moved into a home of our own. God showed us that He had a plan. He opened the windows of Heaven for us again.

Another hurdle that we have encountered is the matter of Glenda's pursuing a career. Could we make ends meet with the disability checks alone? God had shown us throughout His Word that the wife's place of blessing is at home. After an in-depth study of Titus 2, we were confident that the Lord meant exactly what He said in verse 5 that women should be *"keepers at home."* Glenda was never really tempted to return to the school system as a teacher or counselor. However, she was once offered a lucrative opportunity to work as an independent retailer, selling products by giving free facials to stroke patients at a local hospital. The hospital would then consider purchasing their entire line of laundry products from us. The work was to be only one day a week, just a few hours, then expand into two days, and so on.

There was a discussion in our home for several days. I could see the mushrooming effect on her time this job would have. It would take her all morning to dress, get ready and prepare her set-up. Furthermore, the overhead would be no minor expense. When I voted *no*, she reluctantly agreed, but in her heart she knew it was for the best. She admits to privately pouting for a week.

Immediately after that week, God honored her decision to stay home. He poured out financial blessings, over $700—a small fortune in our estimation. It was more than she could have cleared in commissions in a long time. Her role of being a "keeper at home" was forever settled.

Later, after we moved to Lufkin, our two older daughters were enrolled in oil painting lessons (a gift from Glenda's mom). But the class demanded a never-ending list of brushes, canvases, and paints. How would God provide for these? He is so creative. At that same time, a need arose in the home school circle for someone to teach sewing. Our daughter Kimberly, nine years old at this time, had become the little seamstress because of Glenda's teaching, making doll clothes and helping sew her own clothes, so for Glenda to become a sewing teacher seemed to be a natural step. Over the next couple of years Glenda taught girls in our home in the afternoon. Funds were now available for the art supplies as well as her own projects. God rewarded her obedience to His word. Our children learned teamwork and our home training was enhanced!

I have shared these incidents in terms of measurable dollar amounts. But there is an even greater reward in walking with the Lord. The liberty He gives is priceless. Paul wrote in Galatians 5:1, *"Stand fast therefore in the liberty wherewith Christ hath made us free, and be not entangled again with the yoke of bondage."* True prosperity comes only from God as he gives us the freedom to detach ourselves from the temporal and look to the eternal. We can agree with Paul again that *"Godliness with contentment is great gain"* (1 Timothy 6:6).

Gratefulness is a quality that the Lord has produced in us. When we were trying to make things work on our own, we were always wanting more. We were never satisfied with what we had. He used my years of physical disability to chip away our pride. We thank God for the many ways He has transformed our lives. Contentment is a precious gift that He gives. Leaning on Him has become easy. Expecting Him to direct our path has become our way of life.

CHAPTER NINE

GREATER THINGS

By Ron

In the months following the return of my memory, I was often asked to share my entire heavenly experience. I found myself constantly reliving what I had witnessed in Heaven and focusing on the supernatural. Even with my conservative background, I knew firsthand that spiritual gifts and miracles had not passed away. In small steps, the Lord led us to a vibrant Christian fellowship. The expanded time for singing praises, allowing the Holy Spirit's leading, blessed my heart. Glenda and I were constantly stretched spiritually and enlightened as we studied Acts, chapter 2 and beyond.

We learned how Jesus taught the believers to come together through the guidance and power of the Holy Spirit in the absence of His physical presence. The spiritual gifts, as listed in I Corinthians 12, are vital for our very survival. Paul wrote that we shouldn't be ignorant or uninformed in this area. Verses 4 through 11 name the nine gifts and help us understand their extreme importance, *"Now there are varieties of gifts, but the same Spirit. And there are varieties of ministries, and the same Lord. And there are varieties of effects, but the same God who works all things in all persons. But to each one is given the manifestation of the Spirit for the common good. For to one is given the* word of wisdom *through the Spirit, and to another the* word of knowledge *according to the same Spirit; to another* faith *by the same Spirit, and to another* gifts of healing *by the one Spirit, and to another the* effecting of miracles, *and to another* prophecy, *and to another the* distinguishing of spirits, *to another various* kinds of tongues, *and to another the* interpretation of tongues. *But one and the same Spirit works all these things, distributing to each one individually just as He wills."* (NASB).

We fully understood the seven motivational gifts of prophet, teacher, organizer, server, giver, exhorter and mercy as outlined in Romans 12:6-8. As complex creations with God-given personalities, we each approach situations and people differently. Through many sermons, revivals and seminars we had heard these roles clearly defined. But on the subject of *spiritual gifts—the manifestations of the Holy Spirit*—we were newly enlightened.

I marveled at the working of the Holy Spirit and how He has brought forth His supernatural gift in my life. At first, in the new environment of worship, I doubted the energy of the Holy Spirit. At the close of most services, the pastor would invite anyone with a prayer need to come forward. With his hands outstretched, he would pray for each individual. Some began to weep, others began to laugh, still others fell stiffly to the floor. I had never seen such a performance. I mentally fought against what I did not understand and intended to correct the pastor for allowing such acting and emotionalism in the membership. Then one Sunday the Lord dealt with me concerning this.

I stepped out into the aisle to confront the pastor when I felt God's power surge throughout my body. Grasping the rows of chairs, I struggled to maintain my balance and lumbered back to my seat. Shocked, I confessed to Glenda, "God's presence is real!" I immediately repented of my misconceptions and unbelief.

Not long afterward, the Lord allowed me to see angels filling the church, singing and worshipping along with the congregation. What a divinely breathtaking spectacle. I finally composed myself enough to nudge Glenda and whisper, "Angels are everywhere!" The first song of praise was upbeat and joyful. The angels were dancing and moving rapidly; they were so numerous that I was intrigued how they were not bumping into each other. Their lavish, glowing garments draped bodies absent of wings. Each face intensely focused praise to the Father. The very next song was an immediate change of pace to a slow tempo, quiet and reverent. The angels instantly dropped to a kneeling position with their arms raised to the Lord. I witnessed the greatest, most amazing display of worship. In complete awe, I stood wide-eyed, captivated by a divine army of heavenly beings!

For at least forty-five minutes, the music team led the congregation and the unseen host in worship. As the service proceeded with the sermon, the heavenly bodies were invisible to me, but I sensed their presence in the building.

I hesitated to share my revelation but Glenda insisted that I tell the music team. (I had a reverential fear of bringing attention to myself and at the same time, I was not ready to be considered *charismatic*.) Glenda couldn't contain her excitement. The singers marveled at what I told them but they were not surprised. They, too, had felt God's presence in a special way, though not with sight of the heavenly beings.

Why would God allow me this special vision? Would I ever have it again?

The next Sunday couldn't come soon enough. Yes! The angels were back and I couldn't help but raise my hands in praise along with them. My experience incredibly matched David's in Psalm 63:2-4, *"To see thy power and thy glory, so as I have seen thee in the sanctuary. Because thy lovingkindness is better than life, my lips shall praise thee. Thus will I bless thee while I live: I will lift up my hands in thy name."*

With few exceptions, the divine vision is part of my experience every week. The Lord does not force this on me in any way. I truly believe it is a reminder from where He has brought me. My faith is ignited as I partake of this miraculous sight. *Charismatic*, meaning "gifted one," is now a badge of honor.

In the spring of 1995, a pastor friend, Jay Owen, invited us to attend his small country church. Glenda and I arrived late, so we slipped onto the back pew just as the guest speaker was concluding. As he finished his message, he asked a lady to stand and come forward. Courteously, he revealed her special physical and emotional need and prayed for God's intervention in her life. This was prophecy in action, a spiritual gift that, until now, we had not witnessed. Next, a man was singled out who needed healing in his back from an occupational injury. After one or two others, he pointed to *me*! We had driven over an hour and the speaker had come just as far from the opposite direction. How could he know anything about me? The visitor resolutely announced, "God is going to activate His ministry in you very soon. *Your* spiritual gift is to pray for healing and encouragement for others! You must ask the Lord for understanding and for His manifesting this gift in your life," he further explained.

After the close of the service, I introduced myself to the guest and asked him lots of questions. I learned that he personally knew none of those he'd called forth—that the words of knowledge and gift of prophecy was wholly from God. Astounded yet bewildered, Glenda and I returned home with a burning desire to seek God's wisdom and direction.

In July, Jay Owen's family visited our home. Their eighteen-year-old son had a vertebra in his neck visibly out of line, causing him great discomfort. Discerning God's gift in me, his mother said, "Ron, place your hand on Jonathan's neck and pray for healing." With little faith, I obeyed. To my shock and amazement, I felt and saw the vertebra move and align with the others! His pain was instantly relieved.

In another instance, one morning Glenda awoke with a severe crick in her neck and right shoulder. (She has suffered with chronic back pain, irritated by mild scoliosis, most of her life.) This morning she was holding back tears. I strongly sensed the Lord telling me to pray for her healing. While the rest of the family slept, we stood in our family room. With my hands on Glenda's shoulders, I pleaded her case to the Lord.

She told me later, "I knew God could heal me instantly if He chose, but I felt nothing at all. I was afraid to turn my head, not wanting to feel the pain and disappoint you. After your prayer, I rigidly walked to the kitchen, poured myself a cup of coffee, and settled in another room. With no one looking, I "tried out" my neck. I looked to the left and then to the right. No pain! I boldly stretched my head up and down and in all directions. What an indescribable sensation! I had felt nothing during the prayer, yet God had healed!"

On October 1, 1995, a guest speaker captivated our attention as he spoke to a full house on Sunday morning at our church. Our pastor introduced Phil Elston as a lay preacher with the spiritual gift of prophecy. After Elston's teaching on Christ's incredible love and plan for us, he allowed time to exercise his divine gift. He and his wife stood together at the front of the sanctuary. Led by the Holy Spirit, they discerned God's message for several individuals. One by one, Phil asked people to stand so he could share a specific instruction or encouragement as the Lord led. One could have heard a pin drop in the filled auditorium! Glenda and I had witnessed such a gift only once before. I was the fourth person Phil addressed! I have repeatedly listened to his message for me on tape: "You're a tall man, not to look down on people, but to look over people. And you have a very caring heart—you watch over your family and you watch over other people. You have a very caring and compassionate heart."

Elston continued, "Let me see your hands. You have healing hands—that's a gift—your hands are meant to heal. It's almost a compulsion with you—it's hard to restrain—it's something you were born for. You've yet to see what God wants to do with the healing in your hands ... The compassion the Lord placed in your heart is pretty compelling. Don't doubt that, Ron. That is something God gave you. It's a powerful thing. (In) your colleagues and peers that are around you, the Lord has established a credible life with you that influences other men in your sphere who don't know the Lord. They see *hopeless* situations, you see *hopeful* situations. I feel like you're going to affect those men in a powerful way for the Kingdom of God."

I was spellbound; Glenda was blotting her tears. Together we knew God was taking us to a deeper level with Him. God was indeed putting a new song in our hearts to praise Him. Our marriage took on new dimensions of ministry.

In this seven-month span, God brought three people to prophesy of the spiritual gift He planned for me. The witnesses echoed each other and confirmed what I was already experiencing.

Since then, God has given me faith to exercise His appointed gift of healing. With so much yet to learn, God's will is my primary focus. I only want to cooperate with the Master's desire, including His divine timing. Furthermore, I've agreed with wise counsel that I obviously can't take credit when people are healed, so I won't shoulder the blame when they're not. This attitude allows me freedom to keep praying, knowing the results are *all* God's.

The Lord graciously allowed the first several people I prayed for to be healed of their infirmities. God honors simple, childlike faith. Nine-year-old Scott had stabbed his eye with a tree limb and was undergoing treatments by the ophthalmologist. The pain was as much as a child could stand. He could not even open his good eye as the piercing light would transfer pain to the injured one. With his eye patched and optimum anesthetic taken, his mother led him into the house where our Thursday night prayer group had assembled. "Scott was so excited to come tonight," his mother related. "He goes back to the doctor tomorrow and he is expecting to read the entire chart." (The doctor was not so hopeful—in fact, he offered only a slim chance of the eye being saved at all.) In the host's living room, several of us gathered around young Scott and his mother. We did all we knew to do—with direction from James 5:14, we touched our hands with olive oil and placed them carefully on the child's head. We prayed fervently and hoped our prayer would be effective as well, as verse 16 explains. After the prayer, Scott's mother thanked us and they slipped out just as they had come.

Our meeting resumed. "Did anything happen?" I wondered. Friday afternoon Scott's mother called us with the report.

Her son sat in the eye clinic's examination room and confidently told the nurse, "I'm going to read the small print today when you take off my patch! Some Christians prayed for my eye last night and God has healed it!" The doctor could not explain what he saw. Scott's eye was perfect! And, indeed, he read the entire chart.

Sunday morning Scott and his mother visited our church so we could see the results of the miracle for ourselves. The boy appeared as if an injury had never happened. God certainly made the praise and worship meaningful that day! We learned the simplicity of trusting Him and obeying His word.

A few months later, our Thursday night group welcomed another visitor. Brian, a dentist from a town deep in East Texas, had vied for Congress and narrowly lost in the final race. Friends in Lufkin looked forward to enjoying a social evening with Brian and his wife, Roxanne, away from the stress of the political campaign. I soon learned that Brian had been suffering all week with shingles and, incidentally, that they had allowed their son to have the car that night, leaving them with their old family truck to travel the 60 miles to Lufkin. Brian and Roxanne had every excuse to skip the Thursday prayer meeting. Despite all obstacles, they came, though Brian stoically sat through dinner and Bible study in great discomfort.

I watched the change in his expression as the lively conversation relating recent miracles and zeal to know the Savior captured his interest and inspired him to trust God for his own healing. He readily accepted being anointed with oil and encircled by his friends for prayer, as I laid my hands on his head.

"Never have I felt such incredible warmth and sense of overwhelming peace!" he said. "The shingles are gone!"

When asked to feel the heat from his head, Roxanne

exclaimed, "He's as hot as a fever." This was God's healing touch! What joy to witness again God's healing power! *He* honors simple obedience and willingness to *receive* His gift.

Equally important to healing, God added the gift of discernment as I pray for others. Often someone tells me his symptoms, then in prayer God shows me the real root of the problem. Sometimes the cause is indeed physical, but often it is spiritual. It didn't take long to find that harboring resentment or anger is probably the most common non-physical cause of an ailment. Through God's mercy, the hurting one can forgive their offender, release the situation to the Lord and receive His grace and healing. The parable that Jesus taught in Matthew 18 stresses the severe consequences of being *"delivered to the tormentors"* when we fail to forgive our brother (verses 34-35).

One of my first opportunities of ministry was such a case. Our pastor's wife brought a friend, Darlene, with a number of unspecified physical ailments, to our home for prayer. Trying to prepare myself, I prayed and meditated on scripture. Psalm 51 kept rolling through my mind. When the women arrived, Glenda and I shared the passage with them. After a time of prayer, Darlene's condition dramatically improved. She confessed how she had fallen under conviction. "I had a quarrel with my oldest married daughter. Her birthday was last week and I withheld mailing her gift. I had brushed the incident aside until now when the Lord brought it to my mind. I know my attitude was wrong. As soon as I repented and surrendered my anger and disappointment to the Lord, He forgave me and I felt His healing touch. I just praise the Lord for His compassion and mercy!"

As I grow more confident in availing myself for ministry, I realize that I am merely a vessel, an instrument for the Lord to work through. Before interceding for anyone, I pray that I would be emptied of self—my thoughts, expectations, ambitions—any motive that would hinder the Holy Spirit's work. Psalm 51:10 continues to be my personal plea, *"Create in me a clean heart and renew a right spirit within me."*

At times, the discernment the Lord gives is the need to bind and cast out Satan and his evil agenda. Then this is the prerequisite for healing to take place. Our church hosted a financial seminar in February, 1997. On crutches following a complicated hip and leg injury, Don, a middle-aged lawyer from Houston, had been encouraged to attend. At the noon break on Saturday, my friend, Bob Walker, and I took initiative, with Don's permission, to bring his condition before the Lord.

"My doctor has said that I will need two or three more surgeries to reset the pin in my hip and straighten my right leg," Don explained. "I imagine it will always be shorter than my left leg."

Bob and I knelt at Don's feet and began to pray. Then Don admitted, "I'm constantly afraid I'm going to fall and that I'll be crippled for the rest of my life."

This was our clue from God. Hearing that, Bob discerned, "Don, are you aware that this *spirit of fear* is not of the Lord?" Bob and I bound the evil spirit and prayed for healing. In the next moment, we all three witnessed the miraculous! Don's twisted right leg straightened and lengthened as our hands were on it. Don stood aghast. Bob and I almost fainted; we were numb with amazement. Don quietly took a few steps without his crutches. But he cautiously reserved his feelings until his orthopedic doctor could confirm the miracle.

The following Monday morning, upon seeing the new X-ray his doctor exclaimed, "What have you done? The pin is more deeply set and in an excellent position. No further surgery is needed. Use the crutches while your muscles gain strength." Don was elated to find that his legs measured the same.

Don called again on Tuesday, still basking in his healing and grateful for every aspect including his new freedom to stand in the shower. His voice was dancing as he chimed, "I can't believe God would do this for me. He is so good!"

Furthermore, I have learned to pray for the Lord's covering and protection for myself. Many times as we allow the Lord to perfect our giftings, the enemy assaults us. It is a good thing that Glenda is most often at my side as my helpmeet, asking the Lord to cover me with His divine protection.

A few Sunday mornings ago Glenda and I were serving the Lord's Supper in church. Paul and Brenda, a faithful couple in our fellowship, were next in line. We soon found that Paul was suffering from allergies. "I've been to my doctor and even doubled my prescriptions and nothing has worked all week," he moaned. "I need help!" I placed my hand on Paul's head and started to pray. In a few minutes I realized this was more serious than I expected—I was suddenly in the midst of a spiritual battle. Unknowingly, Paul must have given the enemy access. My hand became immobilized to the back of Paul's head and then a sharp pain hit me from behind.

Alert to this, Glenda immediately changed her focus to protect me. "Cover your servant, Lord. Let nothing enter except what comes through You," she prayed. "In the name and through the blood of the Lord Jesus Christ, I ask You, Father, to protect and shield Ron from any evil spirit. Bind and cast this one off that is now buffeting him." In a short moment, my pain was gone as well as Paul's.

With tear-filled eyes, he took a deep breath. "I have not been able to breathe deeply for so long," he confessed. "My head was completely blocked. I don't know how I let the enemy in, but 'Thank you, Lord!—You took care of it'."

When these onslaughts occur, we must remember Whom we serve. Our Lord Jesus Christ nullified Satan's attacks with the Word of God, recorded in Chapter 4 of Matthew. His authority and victory is settled forever as I John 4:4 states, *". . . Greater is He that is in you that he that is in the world."*

I find that God is so creative as He ministers to each person so uniquely. Recently, while Glenda and I prayed for Bonnie, a member of our church, the Lord abruptly stopped me in mid-sentence. Embarrassed, I apologized to her and asked aloud, "What is it Lord? Tell me what's wrong!"

In the next instant He answered me, "Her covering (her husband) is not here. She'll be healed when he is present." I explained to her what I had heard. A few hours later she was back with her husband, Ronald, in our living room. With little deliberation, we all stood and got down to the business of prayer. Her relief came quickly. Bonnie's tears turned to joy as she fell into her husband's arms. The real miracle was how the Lord blessed their marriage, establishing Ronald as the spiritual backbone of his family. Glenda and I give all the glory to the Lord. We cannot praise or thank Him enough and those that come for prayer do the same.

I never fail to be astonished, amazed and joyous at seeing God's healing power. I always desire to seek the Holy Spirit's leading me into all truth, as Jesus Himself explains in John 16:13, *". . . When He, the Spirit of truth, is come, He will guide you into all truth . . . and He will show you things to come."*

God is revealing His desire to restore families. Following a recent out-of-town church service that I was asked to lead, several parent/child pairs came for prayer together. Listening to their requests, the Lord directed a specific answer for each one. After a brief prayer, I realized the Lord wanted one father to pray for his grown daughter himself. I told him, "Sir, the anointing is on you to pray for your daughter." Their tears and tender embrace told me I had not missed the mark. God brought harmony to their home in that moment.

To the father of an asthmatic twelve-year-old daughter, the Lord instructed me to relay that the dad must pray for his child seven mornings, before the family arises. I was eager to hear the result. At times, physical healing is simply the "icing on the cake" when God is performing a work of restoring and renewing *His* family.

While Glenda and I are newly ministering in this direction, we are encouraged that the goal of the church body is to unite in seeking the Holy Spirit to reveal and activate the gifts of the spirit.

With wisdom our pastor affirms, "Christ is the head and we are the individual parts, no one more or less important and no one exalting himself above another—everyone's gifts unique and necessary for the benefit of all."

"Greater things will you do when I am gone" (Paraphrased from John 14:12) would have been a blasphemous statement had Jesus not said it Himself! It is only through many individuals denying self and taking on Christ's commission that collectively we can be the church that He purposed, and do greater things!

CHAPTER TEN

THE RESTORATION CONTINUES

By Ron

Realizing the importance of developing relationships, our church membership meets in homes on Sunday nights. Sharing each other's lives—the failures and successes alike—have knitted us together as family. We make time for singing, Bible study, discussion and prayer, with a focus of ministering to the needs of individuals.

One Sunday evening, Glenda quietly shared with our friend, Bob Walker, that I seem to drag through some days, despite my restored memory and absence of headache. Assuming diabetes was at the root of my health problem, Bob suggested a new approach.

"Ron," he said, "since God has given you the gift of healing, let *me* sit in the chair in your stead while you pray." What a novel plan! We had occasionally *stood in* for someone not present, usually a friend or family member from a distant town, but had never created a situation like this.

Bob took his seat and our group gathered around. Bob prayed first and then I spoke only a few words when the Holy Spirit literally knocked me out.

"You are *not* to do this," a voice thundered in my spirit. I remained unconscious for a number of minutes. I knew I had overstepped my gift and displeased the Lord for praying for myself.

When I awoke, I slowly came to my feet and soon realized that I had a burning sensation in my lower abdomen. Bewildered, I wondered where one's pancreas is located. Could mine have possibly been touched to relieve the diabetes? Only time would tell.

I found a medical chart of organs which educated me that my pancreas is not below the waist. Somewhat embarrassed, I still could not explain what had happened. Curiously, day by day I felt better and had more energy. At the end of the week, I ultimately realized that the unspoken ailment of a spastic colon had been removed from me. I confided in Bob that I had lived with this problem for over twenty years. Like a brother, he rejoiced with me over the new freedom I felt.

Why God healed this infirmity I cannot answer. But I am certainly grateful that He did! I do know that the instruction of James 5:14-16 applies to me as well as everyone else: *"Is any sick among you? Let him call for the elders of the church; and let them pray over him, anointing him with oil in the name of the Lord"* (verse 14).

My pastor has taught that the (supernatural) gifts of the spirit are for the benefit of others, not intended for personal use. I must come to God in faith, confessing my faults and submitting to the church just as He prescribed. I thank the Lord for teaching me this lesson early. And I praise Him and thank Him for making me light on my feet at a time when I am about His business more than ever before. God's ways are awesome and unspeakable. Psalm 145:3 expresses it well, *"Great is the Lord, and greatly to be praised; and His greatness is unsearchable."*

Rain clouds cleared on the following Saturday the day our neighborhood garage sale was scheduled. What a welcome sight was the clear blue sky! Glenda and I were up early as we hoped to liquidate the surplus "treasures" from our house. We happily anticipated the fellowship of the leaders' dinner meeting at our church that evening to close out a busy day.

"Linen tablecloths—volunteer waiters—a gourmet meal with a finale of chocolate cheesecake!—What have we done to deserve this?" I mused to our friends around our elegant table for six. The plates cleared and the coffee served, our church's music team began. Cara Johnson played the piano as her husband, Derron, led one of the pastor's favorite praise tunes. I sang softly, feeling the activities of the day catching up with me.

The tempo quickened into the next song when I suddenly felt a sharp stab in my neck. I swallowed hard. My right hand intuitively went to the spot. Fear gripped me that my shunt tubing somehow had become kinked. Facing me, Glenda instantly became aware of my crisis. I knew by the serious look on her face that she was already interceding for me. Soon Bob Walker was kneeling at my side but my pain intensified. I vaguely heard him say, "I need more men to pray!"

Now writhing in pain, I could not scream for Glenda's sake. "She's been through too much already," I thought, struggling to remain conscious. I hardly noticed as more men gathered around and put their hands on my shoulders and head. "Lord! Have mercy!" my spirit cried out. Derron and Cara raised their voices and instruments in deliberate praise.

Our friend Sara lamented to Glenda, "We can take him to the emergency room. Don't wait too long."

"Thank you, Sara," Glenda whispered, "but this *is* the emergency room!" (Unfortunately, experience has shown us that only the big city "trauma" hospitals offer the expertise that we would need—but I was desperate for relief, and I would have gone.)

Then Bonnie, from several tables away, came to pray at my side. In her prayer language, in the name of Jesus, she took authority over the evil spirit and poured out her heart before the Lord with her hands trembling near the battleground of my neck. At last the attack ended! The pain and pressure in my neck and head ceased.

Exhausted, I heard the Lord tell me to stand. With help from those around me, I eased out of my chair. Next, He commanded, "Raise your right arm." With the music swelling, my arm went up and slowly straightened out toward the ceiling. I was barely cognizant of what happened next. The group witnessed the Lord's taking over.

Glenda wished for a video camera as she later relayed the events to me: "God seemed to stretch and twist your body beyond its six-foot-four-inch frame. With both of your arms now raised, the ceiling tiles appeared to hinder the progress! I prayed on as your position looked painful, yet your expression showed peace."

The intercessors and minstrels continued as God dealt with me. After an eternity of several minutes the Lord released me. My arms came down. My awareness of the surroundings returned. My unrestrained smile signaled victory and everyone cheered. This was "body-life" at its finest!

Well and rejuvenated, I touched my neck again where the pain had been. Stunned, I announced to Glenda, "I can't feel my shunt tubing!" I suddenly realized I had full movement of my neck and head—something I had not had since the surgery in 1982. I rubbed and pinched the right side of my neck and turned my head in all directions. "What *had* God done?" I wondered. The pull of the plastic tubing and restrictions of movement were gone! With tears of joy flowing, Glenda and I hugged each other in the midst of the congregation.

With the season of praise and worship completed, the pastor took charge of the meeting. However, I could not sit down. My energy could not be bottled. I slipped out of the room and actually ran up and down the carpeted hallway, praising the Lord for the relief and freedom He had just given me. I finally rejoined the session and stood at a side wall. I trust my pastor forgave me for my inability to focus on his teaching!

X-rays the following week showed the tubing still in my neck. Without benefit of comparison, it seemed to be more deeply set. I strangely cannot feel the flexible, straw-like tube that was just below the surface, protected in a vein and often visible. Tasks that were once impossible for me are now routine. Raising my right arm to simply change a light bulb formerly jeopardized my health. I would feel the pull and then become lightheaded, with a headache to follow. Praying for mercy and forgiveness for overstepping my limitations, I would wait for the Lord to soothe the pain and stress. He was always faithful. Grateful as I was, eventually I would forget and repeat the process, again and again. It is surprising how many daily tasks require looking up and reaching for something. Now, I praise the Lord every time I have such an opportunity. Glory to God: I am no longer restricted to lift my arms to Heaven to praise His name!

During the writing of this chapter, the phone rang. Our friend, Darlene, had been praying and meditating on the very events I have just related. With divine insight, she heard the Lord direct her to read Isaiah 46:3-4 and to link my name with it. She read from the Amplified Bible over the phone: *"Listen to Me (says the Lord), O house of Jacob, and all the remnant of the house of Israel, you who have been borne by Me from your birth, carried from the womb: Even to your old age I am He, and even to hair white with age will I carry you. I have made, and I will bear; yes, I will carry and will save you."*

Darlene compassionately remembered the pain and torment that I suffered that Saturday night. "The Lord told me to call you right now to remind you that He is protecting your life and that He is in control."

What wonderful encouragement! We laughed at how dramatically God deals with me. Darlene concluded, "Ron, God wants to strengthen your faith, as well as ours! We all need each other!" God is about the business of fitly joining us together, making us *His* glorious church.

CHAPTER ELEVEN

WITH GOD, NOTHING IS IMPOSSIBLE

By Ron

I marvel that, after all these years, the speaking invitations continue to come. After expressing my amazement to a good friend, he said, "Ron, Jesus himself said, 'Remember this!' That should settle it! As long as you give God the glory, He wants you to share the story."

Does it ever grow stale or common? Never!

In fact, as I tell you what happened that Sunday morning, I find myself walking back through time, reliving it. I am not excessively emotional, but a supernatural passion wells up in me as I relate hearing my small son's voice—the child I never knew. So often, Glenda is stronger than I and is able to recount this incident to our audience. (After all, she wasn't there!) My eyes still swell with tears as I try to describe Jesus' eyes. I know my voice still takes on the same intonation when I indignantly said to my guardian angel so long ago, "I want to see my wife!"

I was in another dimension—out-of-body, and in the presence of the Lord. Human words are totally inadequate!

I never tire of telling anyone who wants to listen. The experience is as fresh and alive to me today as it was in the beginning. Isn't that just like God!? Fresh and current . . . His Word is living, His truth is never failing. In His presence it's as though time stands still, there is no aging. Maybe this is why He allows me to keep on telling!

The writing of this book is a story worth sharing. Soon after the infamous fish fry, a number of friends enthusiastically suggested that Glenda and I record our trials and victories in book form. In the course of one week, four people separately encouraged us to write.

First Robert, a friend in our church suggested, "Wouldn't it be wonderful if someone could capture the *essence* of your testimony in a book?"

Then Tesa, a member of our Thursday night Bible study, asked, "Do you have something written, like a small book, that I could send to our friends in Houston? I'm sure they'd like to meet you and hear your testimony if they could read about it first."

The third, Paula, our girls' art teacher, received a word from the Lord. "You two should write a book, not to supply an income but to create a vehicle for ministering to people," she explained.

Finally I met with George, a state rehabilitation counselor with whom I had recently interviewed. As my health dramatically improved, I had hoped to find employment. On a follow-up visit with him, I had a chance to briefly explain how God had used my disability to give me spiritual insights. The professional counselor leaned back in his chair and said, "Ron, I've been a Christian for only one year and I'm just beginning to learn about spiritual matters. I don't think you need a job: you need to go home and write the book!" This fourth confirmation from a secular vocational counselor, a virtual stranger to me, got my attention: God had plans for a book!

Our first attempts at writing proved disastrous. We clearly needed help! Help came in the form of suggested reading to experience good writing, and a loaned computer to work with. It didn't take long for the book to be shelved. Our determination seemed taken away, and discouragement replaced hope of ever completing the task. However, God's will prevailed and through much prayer His plan unfolded.

During the Christmas season the following year, a young man in our church who owned a printing press suggested that we write a tract. He would supply the paper, ink and labor at no charge. We were off and running! Surely it wouldn't take much talent to transfer my recorded testimony to a typewritten page. We were wrong. At least six editors got involved, all with good ideas. In the time that the short manuscript was in revision, our friend moved to the West Coast without his equipment. The project failed again.

Another year went by. The flood occurred and the subsequent miracle of God's supplying us with a house, as you have read. After we were fully settled into a new routine, a letter arrived from Wanda Pridgeon, a lady who had interviewed me for a newspaper article several years earlier. She wrote that since the time of our meeting, her husband Les had continued to be inspired by what I had shared. Mr. Pridgeon, suffering from complications from heart surgeries, had died during that time. The counsel he gave to his wife during his last weeks of life was for her to write our story!

We were amazed and thrilled at God's ways and His care for us. We had put the book on the altar so many times that it was out of our minds. Now it became a prayer request again. Thoroughly convinced of God's clear direction, Wanda devoted many hours to prayer and meditation before the three of us met together over tape recorded sessions in her Dallas home. She agreed that capturing the essence was critical. Despite my willingness to cooperate, Wanda found her job challenging.

"Getting you to express yourself and answer the questions that God gave me in my prayer closet is like cracking a black walnut!" she joked. Month by month, the Lord used the work to lead us all to search out His word and stay on our knees in prayer. Wanda wrote the outline and formulated most of the chapters. From a stirring discussion of the children I observed entering Heaven, she drafted the *Tiny Members* chapter. Without Wanda's help and obedience to the promptings of the Holy Spirit, the book would have never happened.

Our son Doug suffered a broken leg in an accident at a restaurant in 1994. Originally, we were grateful for the restaurant's insurance to meet our medical bills, and thrilled two years later when they offered a friendly cash settlement to take him off their liability claims. With a wonderfully healed leg, Doug's contribution to our home was a computer with all the bells and whistles. With this new addition, the Lord enabled Glenda to learn word processing and get more involved. I am amazed at the writing skills God brought forth in my wife. Of course, the glory is all His for supplying a steady stream of miracles and occurrences worth sharing.

God brought many people into our lives throughout the writing who have all added an integral part. Mary Dunn donated hours of her time with pencil and pad in our living room. From this, God revealed the analogy of Adam and Eve to my hospital introduction to Glenda. The Lord directed talented friends to edit the work more than once. Bob Flournoy who hosts the Thursday night prayer group gave much attention and prayer to the project. Once, an interim manuscript was read aloud, then placed in the center of the group and prayed over. In the final stages before printing, we thanked our pastor and his wife for their continued support and asked them to review our work.

"We understand the importance of being under spiritual authority and welcome your critique and discernment," we told them. Their encouragement and hearty approval affirmed the direction the Lord was taking us.

Our desire throughout has been to seek God's will and bring glory to Him. The end result, like the entire process, has been totally in His hands. We are blessed and reminded daily that ". . . *with God, nothing shall be impossible!"* (Luke 1:37).

It is our hearts' desire that you have been encouraged as we've guided you along some of the paths our lives have taken. Know that your life, as ours, is ordered by the Lord. God's love is great. He places angels around us, nurtures infants in Heaven, hears and answers our prayers, and pours out spiritual gifts to His body of believers for the benefit of us all. Through Jesus Christ alone can we experience life in its fullest—now and throughout eternity. Be assured that Heaven is REAL!

PART II

2016

by Glenda

FOREWORD

A DIVINE CONNECTION

My husband Bill and I have been blessed to know the Petteys for over a decade now. I first met Ron and Glenda Pettey at a healing workshop that was going on in their town. After reading their book, *Heaven Is Real*, I requested a private prayer session for an illness I struggled with at that time. It was at our first meeting where the Lord spoke to me and said that meeting the Petteys was a "divine connection." The truth is that our first meeting began a lifelong friendship full of love, laughter and healing.

I was blessed to watch the Petteys minister on several occasions and always marveled at how God worked through their prayers. Sometimes Ron had specific directions from the Lord for people; other times God just healed them on the spot. People with all kinds of backgrounds and all kinds of conditions received a special touch of the Lord when they came to Ron and Glenda for ministry. As a couple, the Petteys worked well together, complementing each other's unique gifts. When Ron was at a loss for words or direction, Glenda always had them. They were kind and patient with the many suffering people they encountered, and never once did I ever see them ask for any type of compensation. They had servant hearts and enjoyed connecting with people and using the gifts the Lord had entrusted to them. They were the same in private as they were on stage doing ministry—simple, loving and always wanting to shine the light of Christ.

Ron had a gift, one that was not common in the Body of Christ, and that worked in a special way. He was a quiet man who, once you got to know him, was a little mischievous. He had a great sense of humor and always had the look of someone who knew the running inside joke. Ron loved to laugh, especially if he was laughing at himself. After his time in Heaven, he returned with a more childlike demeanor and innocence. He was introspective, often getting quietly lost in his thoughts about his experience, yet was always eager to share his story and pray for those in need.

Even though I knew he suffered with complications from severe diabetes and eventually multiple sclerosis, in all my years of visiting with the Petteys I never once heard him complain. In fact, I can't think of one time when Ron wasn't smiling or was feeling sorry for himself.

Ron lived life with one foot on earth and one foot already in Heaven. His time in Heaven really changed his perspective on life. The mundane, and even at times, serious issues of life did not seem to bother him. Even his own failing health did not appear to concern him. He was preoccupied with God's perspective, and when faced with a crisis would typically smile and say "Hallelujah! Praise the Lord"—his own special code for "No worries, God has it!"

Over the years, I watched people in mainstream ministry bypass Ron to speak because of his physical limitations. I saw that though they had some understanding, they had not yet learned this truth: that God still uses the weak things of this world to show his strength and to shame those who think they are wise. He still hides His treasures in jars of clay. Ron was one of God's special treasures hidden in a jar of clay. He was not suave. He was not a great preacher, an enticing evangelist or an incisive prophet. He was simply a vessel that allowed the kingdom of Jesus to flow through him. He was a simple, quiet man who knew that the most important thing in life was always being in the continual presence of Jesus Christ. The ministry that God allowed Ron to do was always secondary to this.

Even though Ron is now at home in Heaven, his legacy of simple trust and joy in Jesus lives on in the lives of those who were healed and those whom God allowed him to touch. I am grateful to have been one of the special few who got to be a witness to the working of God's grace and healing through his life. As Ron would say, "Hallelujah! Praise the Lord!"

—**Mignon Murrell**, Producer, Alegria TV

PREFACE

R on Pettey was a loving husband and father, connected to his wife and children, ever cognizant of their feelings and discerning of their needs. Yet I want to clarify that he was, indeed, *human* with a normal temperament and frustrations. In our forty-three years of marriage, we rarely had an argument, but we did have frequent "discussions!" Most of those discussions were resolved with Ron convincing me of his opinion, which generally proved to be right.

Ron's parents exhibited teamwork in virtually every area of their lives which surely influenced his view of marriage. Shopping for clothes, cooking and even cleaning house became joint activities. And Ron loved to invite friends to our home. Making burritos for a Mexican buffet made entertaining financially possible in the years our children were young.

Ron was given great gifts at a great expense. True friendships were precious and rare, though he had an abundance of wonderful acquaintances. After his near-death experience in 1982, anyone connecting with Ron would have to meet him on a spiritual level, as the regular gamut of current events, politics and small talk were not in his repertoire. On the surface, Ron may have appeared simple-minded and socially lacking, but those who chose to engage him in purposeful conversation found otherwise. Included in this book are narratives from some of those who knew him well.

Some felt that Ron's ability to "see" into the spiritual realm was God's original intent for mankind, which had been lost because of sin in the Garden of Eden. Ron had made a trip to Heaven and was allowed to bring back a measure of the gift God had intended for everyone. For me and so many others, Ron was our window into the unseen world. What a treat for Ron when he could corroborate with others who could also *see*!

Ron and I witnessed many healing miracles. We spoke of those events in our first book, on our website and in conversations everywhere to give glory to God. They are all the "testimony of Jesus, which is the spirit of prophecy" (Revelation 19:10). The miracles of Jesus can be duplicated; what He does for one, He'll do for you! The miraculous stories of the Bible are our stories! God is looking for agreement on earth—for us to stand on His Word as we declare the truth that He is the same yesterday, today and forever. A testimony of a miracle creates an atmosphere where it can be repeated. The Holy Spirit loves hearing what Jesus has done!

Writing this sequel, which covers the eighteen-year interim from our original book's publication to Ron's home-going, brings closure to a life well-lived. Though Ron and I answered hundreds of emails and countless phone calls and spoke to groups large and small, this book details highlights of the rest of the story for all to know.

Today, as the manuscript is nearing completion, I had an epiphany of an event in scripture.

Jesus told his disciple, Peter, to cast his fishing net on the "other side of the boat" where he would find a huge catch of fish, more than his net would hold. God supplied *what Peter needed*.

Though I have a degree in English, I am not a professional writer.

My spirit heard:

> Cast your net to Me! I will fill it with concepts and words—*what you need* to write this book.
> Words that have Life and will impact many!
> I am a creative God. I create—that's what I do.
> What I put in your net is unique to you!
>
> - Fish for Peter
> - Inventions for some
> - Songs and poetry for others
> - Words and sentences for you
> - Skills and talents beyond your
>   human ability

"Call unto Me and I will answer you, and I will tell you great and mighty things, which you do not know" (Jeremiah 33:3).

INTRODUCTION

During the days after Ron's return to Heaven, the Lord took special care to show me that I was not alone. He had not forgotten me, and He was guiding the circumstances of my life, as usual, proving that the testimony that Ron and I had shared would continue.

We discovered that hydrocephalus, commonly understood as *water on the brain,* was the source of Ron's debilitating headaches. The surgeries to place a shunt to drain spinal fluid caused Ron to become diabetic. We navigated daily through multiple concerns of avoiding further head trauma, blood sugar testing and improving Ron's health in general.

For exactly three years, we owned a wheelchair-accessible van, with the built-in ramp. With the later diagnosis of multiple sclerosis, Ron could travel long past his ability to walk. Now that Ron was gone, I needed to find a regular vehicle.

My beautiful, *like-new* van would not be considered as a trade—I would have the daunting task of selling it myself. My visit to a dealership on a Saturday morning to research my options seemed a bit ambitious and somewhat stressful. When the energetic young salesman asked for my email to follow up, my answer of "rgministries@ . . ." prompted him to ask, "What is the ministry?" I briefly explained that after Ron's near-death experience, we traveled and ministered, and had written a small book. At that very moment, my cell phone beeped. Expecting a message from my daughter, I excused myself to check it. It was a PayPal message showing a book order from *Nottinghamshire, England*. God's sense of humor! The split-second timing of an international order was the comic stress relief I needed!

Only a month or so later a local couple bought my van. What seemed like an eternity at the time was really mere weeks. God knew I still needed our specially-equipped van to transport Ron's power chair and so much more to out-of-town recipients and to bring home my long-awaited comfortable prayer/writing chair. Patience was difficult for me to practice, but in hindsight I saw the folly of my being in such a rush!

With my new chair in place and journal in hand, I began to write. Soon my laptop replaced the journal as I began forming chapters for the new book. By the end of June, a unique phenomenon began to occur. Amazon and PayPal book orders started to trickle in, then continue at a brisk pace. We've shipped books since 1998, though never quite at this rate without some major promotion. So I viewed each order as a hug from Heaven with a nudge to get the sequel written! As I wrote and edited, I had the joy of printing mailing labels to locations across the United States and the globe!

By mid-July, I felt I should take the time to retrieve several dozen email prayer requests that I had not been able to answer in previous weeks. (Through the years, Ron and I had always answered emails, as well as phone calls, to the best of our ability, knowing the needs are real and that the Lord had directed the writers and callers to us.) Today, many of those people are replying with such love and grace. How beautiful to witness the body of Christ supporting each other!

A poignant message from Rodger in Sydney, Australia, is amazingly insightful and so very encouraging. With his permission, I share it here:

Dear Mrs. Pettey,

Thank you, so much, for your reply. I greatly appreciate it. And, thank you for the direction in prayer and repentance you've provided us, in wisdom and through experience.

I am particularly thankful to you, given the seasons of mourning and celebration that you and your family are experiencing at this time with the passing of your beloved husband, Ron.

Mrs. Pettey, although I have never met you or your husband, please permit me to share with you just a few observations I have made about your ministry together from the internet clips I have watched: You truly moved and spoke together in blessed unity! Although it was he who encountered God and experienced the glory of Heaven whilst on that operating table, after sharing AND entrusting it with you, his dear and precious wife, it seemed he much preferred the full, gentle, pure and loving manner in which you articulated his experience to that of his own.

Ron was nothing less than a blessing to you, as you to him, and together, you brought the gift of healing to the body of Christ in a very loving and unique way.

All glory, honour, thanks and praise to God but blessings upon blessings to you and Ron, we pray.

Yours in Christ, Rodger Kroon and family

CHAPTER ONE

WATCH YOUR HEAD, RON!

During the writing and publishing of our 1998 book, we did not have a clear explanation of what caused Ron to have headaches leading up to brain surgeries.

Since then, we have learned that Ron's hydrocephalus resulted from a blow to his head while serving in the Navy in January 1971 during the Viet Nam conflict. Ron, as the weapons yeoman, helped with an early morning transfer of ammo from another ship. Under high winds and miserable sea conditions, the pallet broke and in the process a live shell struck Ron's head and knocked him out. After regaining consciousness but without a corpsman onboard, he simply went to lie down on his bunk. About two weeks later, docked in Hong Kong, Ron had orders from the new corpsman for an X-ray to determine the extent of his concussion. The X-ray was done on the carrier docked alongside, but the medical report was never received back at his ship. By the spring of 1971, Ron's two-year tour was up and, despite his constant dull headache, he was ready to go home!

With the diagnosis of hydrocephalus in December 1978, the neurosurgeon asked, "When did you have the blow to your head?" The only possible answer was the mishap on the ship seven years earlier.

For the next fourteen years following brain surgeries, Ron repeatedly bumped his head which was so tender with scars. Overhanging kitchen cabinets, an open car trunk and even a wall seemed to get in his way.

"Ron, you weren't even close to that cabinet! How did you manage to sway over and crash into it?" Ron's slim six-foot-four height seemed to work against him. It looked as if something strange was behind these episodes. When he regained consciousness after one hard hit, he claimed, "Some invisible force pushed me!"

The most severe event came in early January 1996. Helping me take down the small Christmas tree, Ron knelt beside it. He toppled over, slamming his head against the wall. He was unconscious longer than ever before. I prayed fervently, then called the church to ask whoever answered to pray before I called 911. When the paramedics arrived, Ron had just regained consciousness. They were deliberately slow and cautious to assess his condition. As the minutes passed, they suggested that I could take Ron to the ER, instead of transporting him by ambulance.

The hospital was across town. With the delay of every stop sign and red light, Ron became more alert. Then we were stopped at a train crossing, giving Ron even more time to recover. As we finally approached the turn-in to the ER, we decided that it made more sense to drive on to the church for prayer. Ron had had so many emergency trips with his shunt and diabetes that we cautiously weighed our options before committing to the tedium of the ER.

As we pulled into the church parking lot, our pastor and senior elder were dashing out, coming to meet us at the hospital. They assisted Ron out of our vehicle and into the church. With the four of us standing in the pastor's office, I gave the men a quick explanation and they burst into prayer. After one sentence in English, both men erupted into their prayer language. Although still somewhat new to us, tongues seemed perfectly appropriate in this emergency. In mere moments, Ron interrupted with a clear, strong voice shouting, "What just happened? Something fell from my neck! I felt like I was being choked!" Grabbing his t-shirt under his polo, Ron reenacted how it felt like the shirt suddenly loosened and stretched away from his neck.

What a demonstration of the Lord's victory over evil that day! The years-long pattern of head injuries ended in that moment. The battle had been won, but the war would not end for Ron for a long twenty years more, when he would surely hear the Lord say, as He spoke in a parable, "Well done, my good and faithful servant . . . Enter into the joy of your master" (Matthew 25:21).

Shipmates tossing live shells overboard

CHAPTER TWO

THE GIFT OF SEEING

1949	Ron is born
1970-71	Ron serves in the Navy
1973	Ron receives Jesus
1973	Ron marries Glenda
1978	Ron's first brain surgery, resulting from head trauma in 1971
1982	The brain surgery that takes Ron to Heaven
1992	The fish fry event where Ron's memory is restored and headache healed
1998	*Heaven is Real* is published
2016	Ron's destiny is complete: he enters Heaven to stay

Following Ron's surgery in 1982, for Ron and me the supernatural gradually became more natural, though never taken for granted. It began with the very uncomfortable vision of seeing people in church either glowing with a bright light, or covered in a dark shadow. Later, Ron would see an identical-looking man alongside a speaker at an event. The *twin* was the guardian angel. Then, following prophetic utterances that Ron had a gift of healing, a church member came for prayer. Ron pointed to her heart, noticing that the rhythm seemed off. "Ron, you're seeing it?" "Yes," he stated, as if it were normal. *Shocking*, was my reaction!

The gift of seeing developed into a supernatural MRI/X-ray ability. Ron would commonly notice someone's blood flowing too slowly, even slowing at a major joint, such as the knee. He would see a particular organ highlighted, if that was the part needing repair. The Lord either shone a bright light on the skin's surface or revealed the internal organ, taking the guesswork out of the equation for Ron!

Once, Ron pointed out a spot on a lady's shoulder, saying, "There's the problem. It's *doubt!*" Unexpected and ridiculous as it was, it wasn't denied. The lady repented and her pain left.

"Look at that! Glenda, I know you can see that!" he would say. What I did see was a much healthier, happier individual after the Lord's touch. Ron frequently put his hands over my eyes and prayed, "Lord, open her eyes!" With no change in my vision, he was disappointed that he had to carry this gift/burden alone. On a ministry outing, a pastor's wife quipped, "It's okay that Glenda doesn't 'see' ... hey, someone's got to drive!"

I remember a time when our church's hardworking maintenance man, Don, came to the church in distress. He had been in a traffic accident on his bicycle and had hurt his shoulder. He explained to us that when he went to the doctor about it, the doctor told him he had cancer in the shoulder. We gathered around him in great concern to pray for him, as he was visibly shaken by this news. Ron, however, stood back, looking, shaking his head—no. The rest of us were comforting Don, praying for healing, and rebuking the cancer, but Ron kept saying quietly, "It's a lie, it's a lie, the cancer is a lie." Finally we stopped praying and asked Ron what he meant. He just shrugged his shoulders and repeated, "This cancer is a lie."

A few days later, Don came in, looking sheepish. "Oh, those foreign doctors," he said, "I can never understand their accents. I misunderstood what he said. He told me if I didn't take care of my shoulder, there was a possibility I could develop cancer there—I don't actually have cancer."

What Ron was saying hadn't made sense to us while we were praying for Don. But later we realized that Ron had been seeing the reality—there was no cancer there.

Ron had an innate reverence about this gift—he was in awe of the Lord's allowing him to see and at the same time, guarded not to appear foolish. On the other hand, I was intrigued and clamoring to know more. "Ron . . . What are you seeing? What is the angel doing? What is he wearing? Can you speak to him?" My enthusiasm overwhelmed him and sometimes caused him to retreat. As I matured to grasp the weight of his gift, I grew into an asset rather than a liability for Ron.

On one glorious occasion, a new friend invited us to a service where he was to be the guest speaker. The one-night event was held in a high school auditorium and was jointly hosted by several churches. As the meeting began, Ron noticed grotesque figures plastered to the walls of the auditorium. He discreetly whispered to me, "Glenda, I've never seen this before! It appears that demons are flattened and stuck along the walls!" Concealing my shock, I instantly had a revelation. "Ron, I believe you are seeing the result of the prayer coverage—the intercession prior to this meeting! Those demons reside here—the intercessors didn't have authority to demand them out, but only to subdue them for this occasion." Could it be that Ron was seeing a virtual display depicting the authority Jesus gave us to "bind on earth?" (Matthew 16:19)

I further questioned Ron, "Do they have an identity— can you see a name?" Ron prayed and suddenly he saw banners appear across their chests. "I'm seeing the names now . . . 'lust,' 'pride,' 'doubt'." We kept pleasant expressions as we both prayed for God's protection in the meeting and that the audience would be completely unaffected.

At the close of the service, we were invited to join with the prayer teams. The leader directed us to pray individually, rather than as a couple, to accommodate the crowd. The Holy Spirit seemed to be working overtime! The Lord gave us accurate assessments as we counseled and prayed while He visibly touched the recipients.

From living rooms to small country churches to large auditoriums, Ron shared his story with vigor, which was quite a feat for a man with normally slow, halted speech! By the fall of 1998, with the book in circulation, we began receiving strangers into our house. The formal living room became our prayer room. Eventually, we moved the prayer sessions to a room at our church. People called to make appointments, drove to our town or flew into a major airport with yet another two-hour drive to reach us.

Long prayer lines followed every service. Though Ron preferred to spend time with each one, speediness was required. At a large church in Georgia, we conducted a two-hour service and then met with hundreds in a ten-hour line! We had walked in at 10 a.m. and out at 10 p.m., yet back at our hotel at 11:00 that night, we marveled to each other how we were not tired!

Sometimes the emotional, personal needs were greater than the physical. On a Sunday morning in St. Louis, Missouri, I kept an eye on the clock to allow time for prayer. I believe the entire congregation wrapped around the outside aisle of the church. As they came to us on the platform, one by one, they each mentioned a medical need, yet their eyes all revealed a deeper longing . . . they were starved for a personal touch from the Lord—they yearned for an affirming hug from the Father. We became His listening ears and His outstretched arms that day.

At a ministry outpost in Arkansas, buses arrived with men from a rehab camp joining the regular members. Since the men had a curfew to return to the camp, we stayed on the platform while they filed by for us to have a point of contact with each one. God gave a word of encouragement and direction for each man through His servant, Ron.

For Ron, so much fun was seeing the angels. Auditoriums were overflowing with them—hundreds, even thousands. Ron marveled at how they were all moving and dancing without bumping into each other!

Back in Arkansas, a prophetic dancer named Jessica wearing a long, flowing dress performed a beautiful interpretive dance. Ron was astounded as he watched Jesus, Himself, join her. From that night on, Ron glowed as he recalled Jesus dancing with Jessica!

Often, almost daily, Ron saw two larger-than-life angels standing in the doorway to our bedroom. One held a journal and a pen, and was always writing. Though Ron never conversed with them, we felt the angelic activity correlated with the passage in Malachi 3:16: "Then those who feared the Lord spoke to one another, And the Lord listened and heard them; So a book of remembrance was written before Him For those who fear the Lord and who meditate on His name."

One single, very tall angel on assignment stayed in our foyer. Even in the privacy of our home, Ron was slow to mention these visions to me. He loved those rare times when friends or visitors could confirm what he saw, even though they might only see a silhouette, a glow or simply discern the presence of a heavenly being.

From freeing people from the addiction of cigarettes to healing from disease, God chose to work through Ron. Always in awe and gratitude, Ron frequently heard the Lord remind him, "Ron, stop *thanking* Me so much . . . just be obedient!"

Staff photo by Bronwyn Turner

RON AND GLENDA Pettey spoke Thursday to a Stephen F. Austin State University psychology class on Pettey's near-death experience. The class taught by Dr. Joe Kartye, a Lufkin psychologist and adjunct professor, was studying death and dying. Pettey and his wife have written a book about his experience, "Heaven is Real," which should be in area Christian book stores this coming week. A book-signing party is set for Sept. 12 at Christian Words and Works.

The following morning, as doctors struggled to save Pettey, he had his near-death experience. He arrived at a bright place with a large, long table, with a large open book. "I said 'I'm ready to go in,'" Pettey said. "I knew it was

allowed to listen in on one prayer, from the pulpit of a church the Petteys had once attended. After Pettey recovered, the church found a tape of that particular service and his recollection of the prayer matched the actual recorded

time for me to go. I want you to know I'll always be around if you ever need me. Just call upon the Lord."

● Jesus standing at the gate - At the entrance, Jesus called each person by name,

Speaking at the university with our newly released book.

CHAPTER THREE

DELIVERING A SERMON

Speaking of Ron's heavenly encounter was most often the reason for our invitations to meet with groups, small or large. Even on television or radio, everyone wanted to hear about Heaven. On rare occasions, we were asked to return and talk on another subject.

One of those times was especially memorable.

Pastor Charles Burchett called one day and said, "Ron, Beverly and I are going on a ski trip next month. Would you and Glenda like to join us?"

"Thanks, Charles. Sounds like fun, but I don't think I'm up to it now!"

"Well then, Ron, how about you cover for me during the Sunday that I'm out?"

While I was appreciative of the vacation offer, now I was apprehensive for Ron to fill a pulpit . . . they had already heard our story! Ron was calm . . . he would have a month to prepare.

Time passed. The word Ron received was LOVE. Day

by day, the Word was Love—that was it. Ron resisted dictionary help, no books were opened . . . just waiting on that still, small voice to dictate the sermon! He relied on hearing the Lord's voice while in the shower . . . a technique that had worked for him in the past!

The day arrived. We were up early, dressed and ready for the hour-plus drive to the church. The Lord repeated, "Love" . . . nothing else. Ron was driving; I was riding with his Bible in my lap, ready to look up any other key verse to complement "God is Love."

We arrived at the church. Greetings said, the music and announcements over, Ron was up! The congregation was accustomed to a twenty—to thirty-minute message. I felt out of place sitting in the pew instead of standing beside Ron on the platform. I glanced at my watch, ready to time the shortest sermon on record. I was smiling and working hard to avoid cringeing, as it would show so little faith!

Ron opened with a line that I'd given him as an icebreaker. He proudly announced that the message he had was Love. "God is Love." What more can be added? GOD IS LOVE! Ron was not gifted in small talk or using jokes as fillers. For his wife in the audience, this was torture in slow motion! He stumbled for a few minutes as he began to notice that the worship leader's twelve-year-old daughter, sitting alone on the first row, was actually not alone! Her guardian angel was beside her, focused solely on the girl. The angel, without wings, mirrored the image of the girl, similar in height and appearance. The angel seemed oblivious to the surroundings, concentrating on its charge.

Ron transitioned into a twenty-five-minute talk, expounding on how God, in His infinite love, sends personal, individualized servants for His beloved. The *word* became a message, the insight timeless. It was a sermon no one would soon forget!

CHAPTER FOUR

GOD OPENS DOORS

In the early 1990s we studied Henry Blackaby's book, *Experiencing God*. The simple, yet profound theme was that God is always at work around us and invites us to get involved in what He is doing. Week by week, we learned that coincidence and luck do not exist: instead, God is in control. Our job is to *properly respond* to everyone and everything He allows in our lives, while praying that His "will be done on earth as it is in Heaven!"

God weaves divine appointments and divine connections into our lives with a rich deposit of His character and grace. God loves doing this simply because He can.

In early 2000, we found a book order in our post office box, with a generous check, from a woman named Marty. Our thank-you note prompted her to call. Marty was a vivacious, stay-at-home mother of two young boys. A new believer, Marty was on fire for Jesus! After several phone conversations, she asked for additional books and we learned that she was also intrigued with the writings and ministry of Jim Cymbala, pastor of the renowned Brooklyn Tabernacle in Brooklyn, New York. Marty planned a trip to New York to attend the Tabernacle's famous prayer meeting. Cymbala had seen phenomenal growth and success in his church stemming from the humble beginning of a handful of believers gathering on Tuesday nights to pray. God's presence—The Holy Spirit—had erupted in Brooklyn and Marty wanted to feel the touch of God for herself!

Marty hoped to share this adventure with us! On short notice, she booked our flights and hotel rooms for the day after Easter. We met our benefactor on the flight to New York!

With Marty's gift of Cymbala's best-selling book in hand, I brushed up on the history and facts of where we were going. *Fresh Wind, Fresh Fire* would later become my go-to book for inspiration in praying for our own children.

A limousine delivered us from the airport to The Plaza Hotel in Manhattan. Ron and I tried to keep our cool and not act like two kids in a candy store! On Tuesday morning we arrived by cab at the Brooklyn Tabernacle. The entrance on Flatbush Avenue was unassuming compared to the interior grandeur of the 1,400-seat theater that had been transformed into a church.

The day began with a meet-and-greet brunch, followed by a warm, welcoming speech by Cymbala himself. Marty had instructed us to bring plenty of our books to distribute all along the way, especially to the Tabernacle staff. It was a tragic moment for her when she learned that we had forgotten them in our suitcase back at the hotel. Still, Marty introduced us and promoted us as much as conversation would allow.

We were given a roster of the breakout sessions designed to equip church leaders in their specific functions. Around

fifty ministers from all parts of the country were taking
notes and absorbing the vital information to enhance their
jobs back home. Our best times were between the sessions
when we had a few minutes to converse with fellow visitors
or the staff. During a long afternoon break, we became
acquainted with one of the associate pastors and his wife.
Our conversation led to his asking for prayer for himself.
We had found our niche in this event. When we returned
home, we mailed the minister our book. The day ended
with the anointed, massive prayer meeting complete
with the famous Brooklyn Tabernacle choir. During the
service, written prayer requests collected at the church
from week to week were passed down each aisle. Everyone
took a card. With the direction from Pastor Cymbala, the
entire congregation prayed aloud, simultaneously for five
minutes. We could feel the surge of power going into the
throne room of Heaven as God heard every voice.

Back at the hotel that night, we met with Marty, praising
God and praying together to maintain this new level of
worship as we moved forward in our journey with Him.

Only too early on Wednesday morning we had to leave
our posh, twelfth-floor room at The Plaza, with its iconic
view of Central Park, and shuttle back to the airport with
our new Texas friend.

The wonderful extravaganza with Marty taught us that
the Lord has purposes for a reason and a season, just as
Ecclesiastes 3 explains. Getting to know Marty was pure
joy—her exuberance was contagious. Marty shared her
love of Jesus everywhere she went. She told Ron's story
without reservation, without the caution to be *slow* as Ron
had initially heard from the angel. Marty's enthusiastic
support was a sign that God was releasing His anointing of
boldness into our lives.

By midsummer, Marty's husband was offered a

promotion which required a transfer out of state. Though Marty initially resisted the move, she supported her husband and welcomed her next adventure. The *brevity* of this wonderful relationship with Marty was in stark contrast to any we had known. We found comfort in the truth that "God opens doors that no man can open and closes doors that no man can shut." (Revelation 3:7).

We would be reminded of this truth in Revelation again when we were asked to speak on a university campus. One day Dr. Joe Kartye invited us to share our story with his psychology class, followed by a second invitation from a colleague, Dr. Jim Townes in communications. During the discussion after our talk in Joe's class, a student raised her hand to ask, "Ron, wouldn't you *agree* that since God is known as a *loving god* that He will allow everyone to enter Heaven?" I held my breath and looked at Ron. He smiled and without hesitation answered, "Yes, I agree! . . . As long as the person goes through Jesus—Jesus *is* the door into Heaven." The student never looked away. She accepted the answer and even stayed after class to learn more about Heaven and our Heavenly Father.

On one occasion, a student in Jim's class confessed that upon hearing of our coming, he had judged us to be fraudulent, expecting our talk to be invented and without merit. Yet, the moment we walked through the door, that student had an overwhelming sense of the integrity of our message. In fact, he heard the Lord say, "Pay attention! I've sent them to tell you the Truth!" The Holy Spirit went before us, preparing our way again.

Students were encouraged to bring guests to Jim's class on one Thursday. A young man even brought his mother. Our talk and the Q-and-A was lively that day. So lively, in fact, that Jim insisted that we return the following Tuesday to the next class meeting. Tragically, a student's forty-two-year-old father died during the weekend. The mood of the class was somber, but what a testimony to the urgency to know Jesus! The reality that Ron shared of Heaven became personal.

Visiting the classes for almost a decade ended in the same semester—our time was up. God closed the door.

Yet, God demonstrates the beauty of our living, and moving and having our being in Him daily! (Acts 17:28)

Living in a small town has its advantages. Friendships and acquaintances are interconnected where we shop, eat, bank or have business of any sort. In the early months after our book's publication, several store owners and even doctors offered to display the book on their front counters and sell it for us with no profit to themselves. One such business was a stylish dress shop in the mall. Mary, the owner, was intrigued with our story and wanted to share it with her friends and customers, alike. I dropped in periodically, both to shop and check on her small inventory of our book.

Around mid-year 2002, Mary invited us to come to her church where one of NASA's astronauts was to be the guest speaker. We promised to be there! Mary lived and attended church in a lake-side village about an hour's drive from town. With good directions, we were right on time for the Sunday morning event. Mary introduced us to her pastor and several of her friends. Then, the guest of honor arrived and, feeling a little star-struck, we shook hands with Astronaut Rick Husband. Rick was a tall, handsome young father, just as bold and confident of his Christian faith as his aerospace training. He proudly spoke of his upbringing, his college days and the path that led him to where he was now, preparing to be the commander of the upcoming shuttle mission. He gave honor to Jesus Christ, his Lord, for every aspect of his life—his wife and young children, and the destiny to which he had been called.

At the end of his talk, he offered to sign the 8x10" NASA photos of himself that he'd brought with him. Rick signed ours with his signature verse, Proverbs 3: 5-6, which mirrored the talk he'd just given—trusting the Lord with all his heart and confident that God would direct his path. Mary introduced us as authors, briefly telling Rick our background. So, we signed one book for him and one for Mary's pastor as well. Mary had arranged a luncheon and insisted that Ron and I join the group. We were seated at the restaurant's large round table next to Rick and his traveling buddy, the pastor, his wife, and our friend Mary. I cannot recall the conversation—I was overwhelmed at how surreal it seemed to be in this distinguished company.

Fast-forward to Saturday morning, February 1, 2003. We were just coming into the kitchen to make coffee when a loud BOOM literally shook the house. Just one blast and everyone was wondering what it could possibly be! In no time, the tragic news was announced: on its descent, the Space Shuttle Columbia had exploded and disintegrated just north of us. Immediately, I blurted out, "That was Rick's mission! Oh, NO!" We were in shock, along with the entire nation. Yet we knew firsthand of Rick's faith and that he had boldly shared the Lord with his crew. We knew that quicker than in the blink of an eye, Rick was with Jesus. We wondered if Rick had read our book which details the awe and wonder of Heaven and the indescribable peace of being in the very presence of Jesus. Regardless, Rick knew that peace now.

> Trust in the Lord with all your heart, and lean not on your own understanding. In all your ways acknowledge Him, and He shall direct your path.
>
> —Proverbs 3:5-6.

CHAPTER FIVE

A CROSS TO BEAR

Ron found that being the recipient of a healing anointing was quite a load to carry. Ron's gift allowed him to discern root issues in others quite well, but not so much when it pertained to himself. He'd become diabetic from the series of brain surgeries in 1981. Trauma diabetes, the doctors said. He'd endured frequent blood testing and two types of insulin along with a radical change of diet. When his doctor told him he was a *brittle* diabetic, meaning his blood sugar readings bounced from high to low and back up again, Ron took it as a life sentence!

As Ron's healing gift unfolded, it was clear that he, himself, needed healing. We'd heard of diabetes being healed in Third World countries, along with other seemingly impossible issues. (Never mind that Ron had witnessed cancerous tumors disappearing and heart conditions healed!)

Ron was shy, if not stubborn, resisting prayer for himself. Repeatedly, at the close of church services when the call for prayer was offered, I pleaded, "Ron, you should go down to the altar and get prayer!" One day Ron finally revealed the reason for his reluctance to receive prayer: "Glenda, diabetes is my cross to bear!" Our pastor taught that "ideas have consequences" and this misconception was one giant roadblock! I looked for scriptures that could help Ron get past this misconception.

True to Ron's thinking, Jesus had told his disciples, "If anyone desires to come after me, let him deny himself, and take up his cross and follow me." (Matthew 16:24) To follow Jesus would require a personal sacrifice, but suffering a disease surely was not what He had in mind. The Lord conveyed to the apostle John that it was His desire for us, His children, "to prosper and be in good health as your soul prospers" (3 John 2:2). Understanding that Jesus Himself, "took our infirmities and bore our diseases on the cross" should settle the issue once and for all, I told him.

Ron's cross, his mission, was to be obedient to the call on his life. Sickness and disease were not his cross to bear, as Ron mistakenly believed. For Ron to be given the extreme gift of sight was quite a weight for him to carry. Yet Jesus assured us He would help: "My yoke is easy and my burden is light." (Matthew 11:30)

Ron eventually accepted this definition, or at least agreed to satisfy me. Still, at the end of his life, though requiring insulin, his blood sugar labs had improved to levels of a non-diabetic. In our human frailty, God's grace sufficed.

CHAPTER SIX

THE HANDPRINT OF JESUS

By Jan Peterson

I first met Ron Pettey in September 1998, at Christian Words and Works bookstore in Lufkin, Texas, at an advertised book signing. I had previously become acquainted with Glenda Pettey at Christian Women's Club luncheons, where we modeled for the style shows. She was a lovely, friendly woman who seemed sincere and genuine. My first impression of Ron was that he was literally *larger than life*. He was so tall and so serious about his book. He signed the book "Philippians 1:21" which reads *"For to me, to live is Christ, and to die is gain."*

Having met the Petteys, I was eager to read the book. I was fascinated and could not put the book down until I finished. While reading this powerful testimony, my faith was challenged and increased. Afterward, I purchased more books to give as gifts to my family and friends.

In the fall of 2002, my husband Pete and I attended the first Healing Conference, sponsored by our St. Cyprian›s chapter of the International Order of St. Luke the Physician (OSL). Ron and Glenda were there, along with many others from their church. Pete sensed a divine connection with this couple and we became fast friends. As we stayed late to visit on that Friday night, Ron captivated our attention when he confided that he saw angels in our parish hall. Because I had read his account of angels in his book, I listened with great interest. However, the angels he described were not guardian angels or angels that were praising and worshiping; these were large warrior angels. He believed that they were on assignment in spiritual warfare to protect our church, and those who attended the conference, from the assaults of the Enemy. As we talked, we recognized that God had given the four of us the desire to spread the Good News, to encourage the saints, and to pray for God to heal those who were suffering.

Ron and Glenda already had their own healing ministry, which Pete and I supported in prayer and encouragement as it continued throughout the years from 2002 until 2016. They became members of the Order of St. Luke and joined us in our weekly Bible study where we studied the healing miracles of Jesus. We attended other OSL conferences together, eager to learn more about effective prayer.

Ron always prayed with love and compassion. One unique gift that I observed over and over was a gift of discernment that involved Ron's seeing with more than his physical eyes. When praying for a person, Ron would see "inside" the person. He said that the Lord would highlight an area that He wanted to heal. Sometimes this would correspond to the symptoms for which the person had asked for prayer, but often it would be a more serious condition. The person would say, "How did you know?" Other times there would be mental or emotional pain from trauma or a spiritual issue, resulting from sin or confusion caused by the Enemy. When the root of a problem was caused by resentment and an inability to forgive, Ron and Glenda would lead the person in a prayer of forgiveness, resulting in peace. Frequently, the physical issues would clear as well.

On September 11, 2003, my husband suddenly fell ill and helpless one morning at work. He became unable to walk and had difficulty breathing. He felt cold all over, as if his bones were frozen inside him. He was barely able to telephone his son, who immediately came to get him and drove him to the doctor's office. The doctor sent him to the hospital telling me, confidentially, that the only other patient she had seen with his symptoms had died.

When I called Ron and Glenda, they came at once to the hospital emergency room and prayed for Pete. By this time, Pete had an extremely high temperature and had been put on oxygen. He had developed tremors and spasms, particularly affecting his chest and the right side of his body. After prayer, Ron saw what none of us, including the medical personnel, had noticed—a mosquito bite on Pete's right leg. Pete was seen by nine doctors who, collectively, ruled out heart attack, stroke, aneurysm and other conditions. Even though they made no clear diagnosis, they suspected neuroinvasive West Nile virus. Although Pete was put in strict isolation in the ICU, Ron was allowed to see him.

The situation was grim and Ron sensed a heavy weight on Pete's chest. Pete roused to confirm that because of that weight he could scarcely breathe. Ron prayed and in that moment the weight lifted and Pete spoke with a stronger voice. This was the turning point in Pete's recovery. Although Pete was still partially paralyzed when he left the hospital two weeks later, God restored his health.

What a blessing that Pete was strong enough to help

me when I began experiencing alarming symptoms in May, 2009, and then had a biopsy which led to a diagnosis of uterine cancer. I was advised to have surgery as soon as I could find a surgeon and have it scheduled. Since I was a teacher in the final weeks of the school year, I did not want my students or the other teachers—*anyone*—to know. I was paralyzed with fear and dread in the face of such a lethal diagnosis.

After much prayer, I had the courage to share my foreboding news with Ron and Glenda. Ron had a word of knowledge: he told me to eat collard greens. I did so, eating them several times a day. In my subsequent research of cancer prevention and diet, I found that *collard greens* and other green vegetables have been documented as actually killing cancer cells.

At the next Tuesday night OSL meeting, Ron led the group in praying for me. The spirit of fear was cast out. This was the turning point as I began to live in faith that God could heal me of cancer.

In June, I was finally able to talk about my health condition and ask for prayers. I was put on many prayer lists locally and even nationally as saints heard the news and began to pray for my healing. After surgery in June, the surgeon was surprised that there was no large tumor (as he expected from my initial symptoms) and that the cancer had not spread. We rejoiced that the cancer was contained and removed; no radiation or chemotherapy needed. I was cancer-free. Hallelujah!

In the summer of 2010, Pete again began to have trouble walking and became short of breath. His cardiologist diagnosed him with congestive heart failure and scheduled surgery for stents. The night before Pete entered the hospital, Ron and others at the OSL meeting prayed for him. God healed him of a respiratory issue, but the cardiologist found that he needed bypass surgery; the major artery in his heart was ninety-eight percent blocked.

The operation was a successful triple bypass, but complications developed afterward. Ron and Glenda came to visit Pete in the hospital room to pray for him. As Ron stared intently at Pete's chest, he said, "His heart is not in the right place." We were all troubled by this as Ron continued to stare and repeated this phrase with concern and distress. Glenda reminded Ron that when the Lord highlighted a condition, it was because he wanted them to pray for healing. So Ron and Glenda prayed, but afterward Ron said in frustration, "His heart is still not in the right place."

Something amazing happened the next night, on Pete's first night home from the hospital. I awakened to see him next to me in bed with his arms raised in praise and his eyes open, staring up at something I could not see. He was unable to speak, but I discerned he was having a vision. I was at peace and fell asleep again.

He awakened me sometime later and told me that Jesus Himself had come. He repeated what Jesus said to him: "The architects, the electricians and the plumbers have done all they could. Now I will heal you." Then Jesus touched him, laying His hand on Pete's chest. Pete felt his heart move. He knew then he was healed.

Several days later, Ron and Glenda came to visit Pete before they left for a ministry trip to Arkansas. Pete shared his vision. Ron stared at him intently and said that he had been wondering what he had been seeing on Pete's chest since they had arrived at our home. He realized that it was a handprint—the handprint of Jesus!

In 2011, *Heaven is Real* was chosen to be one of the recommended books offered through OSL Resource Office.

On February 21, 2016, the Petteys were featured speakers

in an OSL Tele-Conference Call originating in Canada. Glenda shared their story, with Ron encouraging her.

Finally, Ron's obituary was published in the May/June 2016 issue of "Sharing: A Journal on Christian Healing," the official OSL publication. It ends with the following: "We will miss our dear friend Ron, but are happy for him to return to Heaven, his desire for all these years. His testimony is still available online and through his book, even though God has called him home."

CHAPTER SEVEN

PROPHETIC HEALING FOOD

The gift of knowledge—prophetic insight—came as a surprise to Ron. He eventually overcame the shock of seeing everything! Then Ron began to hear the Lord speak a single word as he was praying for someone. To his surprise, as it came when he prayed for Jan, the word was something to eat or drink. He heard it loud and clear, as if the Lord were shouting it!

With only an average knowledge of nutrition, Ron had no particular thought of a food choice to combat any given symptom. He only repeated whatever word he heard while praying. Over time, the recommended list of fruits, vegetables and liquids grew quite long. Often, the prophetic food contained the nutrients needed for healing. For example, the Lord told a lady with a heart condition to eat sweet potatoes. She obeyed and was happy to report the next day that in her research, she found the sweet potato to have five heart-healthy nutrients. Another time, the Lord advised a small glass of red wine for better blood circulation. As it was not our practice to drink alcohol, Ron stumbled over this one for a bit; finally he just gave the word and stressed moderation. Quite surprisingly, while praying for a woman with a lung problem, the Lord specifically told Ron "white wine!" I searched that one on Google myself! Who knew that the American Thoracic Society had recently determined that white wine was beneficial to the lungs?

During a week-long event held in Branson, Missouri, the Lord clearly directed another woman to eat turnip greens to overcome insomnia. She cheerfully reported back the next day that she had eaten turnip greens at buffets both noon and evening and slept through the night for the first time in months. She continued to eat turnip greens the rest of the week and located us each morning to give us her good report! The *words of foods* were essentially healthy choices, although at times, we wondered if the Lord was healing through nutrition or through testing one's obedience to follow a command, such as in the Old Testament account of Naaman who was told to go dip in the Jordan River seven times to be healed of leprosy.

Once or twice, Ron delivered a word that he'd never heard before. While praying for a friend with a heart condition, Ron said, "I'm getting the word *papaya*." Then, in his next breath and to my embarrassment, he asked, "What's a papaya?" Our friend admitted that he wasn't familiar with the fruit either, but he would cooperate with the Lord's direction and find one. Another time, Ron heard the *unknown-to-him* word, *kumquat*, a fruit even more obscure than papaya.

The Lord recommended both milk and red wine to Linda to manage the intense pain and insomnia from chemo treatments. Linda had experienced a stream of miracles healing her from cancer, but she remained in the care of her oncologists. Linda was willing to try anything, at least for a night, to get relief. She modified her meds to drink a glass of milk, and then later in the evening she enjoyed a small amount of red wine. She called the next day to report the best night's sleep in months, pain-free.

Patrick, whose friendship we cultivated through email and then visits, phoned to ask Ron to pray for his four-year-old daughter. Ron heard, "Give her a big, red strawberry!" While she may have benefitted from that fruit's vitamins or fiber, Patrick beamed: "Ron, I've always called her 'my little strawberry'!"

Ron happened to be watching out a window when our friend Joe dropped in to visit one day. As Joe stepped out of his car and headed to our door, Ron already had the word that *Joe was so dry* and that he desperately needed water. Joe had, indeed, come for prayer. Of all things, his big toe was in great pain. Ron went for a cold bottle of water for Joe's fast relief. As unreal as it is for me to report, Ron watched the water filter down through Joe's system. His toe stopped hurting in just a couple of minutes when the bottle was empty. We discussed how Joe had allowed himself to become dehydrated. He confessed that he never drinks water. His daily routine is to drive to a gas station for a newspaper and chocolate milk on his way to school where he is a coach. Then, for lunch and dinner, he drinks sweet tea but no water throughout the day. Joe vowed to change his habits and praised the Lord for getting him on track.

The long list of prophetic edibles included apples, grapes, fish, tuna, greens, blueberries, pineapple and even once, peanut butter.

Even though Ron was given divine insight to healing, I had to deal with the real world of nutrition to combat Ron's diabetes and eventual multiple sclerosis. Through webinars, social media and any number of resources, I learned more about nutrition and the necessity of healthy lifestyle choices. When I am asked to pray for healing, I often draw upon knowledge that the Lord has given me and/or ask the Lord to quicken a physical appetite for what is needed. It is God's will to heal, but it is also our responsibility to make wise choices. So many times, I've used a simple analogy that we cannot put water in our car's gas tank and expect the car to run. While God is not limited to time and space, it is to our benefit to cooperate with nature, as He designed it.

We are what we eat. And, to quote the cow on the organic yogurt label, *"You are what I eat!"*

CHAPTER EIGHT

THE POWER OF OUR WORDS

Months before our daughter's wedding we were searching for a larger dining table to accommodate our growing family. At a local furniture store, our conversation with the salesman, Jim, evolved into sharing our faith. We became aware that our mission was more than shopping for a table and we offered him our book.

Jim beamed with excitement and curiosity as he received our small gift. We eventually found a table elsewhere and heard nothing back from him . . . until two years later. Jim called one morning with a frantic prayer request. He explained that his wife Sara had been up all night praying for her mother, who was awaiting surgery for cancer. Through her tears and anguish, she had gazed at their bookshelf and had been drawn to our little green book. Waking her husband in the middle of the night, she held the book in front of him and demanded, "Where did this come from?" Jim groggily answered that he had shown it to her a couple of years earlier and then dozed back to sleep.

Sara stayed awake the rest of the night reading. By morning, she insisted that her husband call us. Later that day they both called, and we spent a long time praying with Sara on the phone and encouraging her. Finally, Ron boldly declared that Sara's mother's cancer was gone! Sara was relieved and full of faith that God had healed her mother. When we hung up, I pleaded with Ron that he should have softened his answer and not been so bold to declare the cancer completely gone. Ron replied, "Glenda, I can only say what the Lord is showing me. I saw it leave. The Lord took out the cancer and healed her!"

Time passed. We didn't hear from the couple. Finally, many months later, we called the store with a furniture question. As soon as I spoke with Jim, he began relating the events of his mother-in-law's surgery. He told how the cancer was *still present* at the time of surgery. The doctors had warned the family of a difficult and lengthy surgery, as well as an extensive recovery time. They had warned them not to expect the matriarch of their family to be able to prepare meals for Christmas, much less for Thanksgiving.

On the day of surgery, the doctors had returned to the waiting room to speak to the family hours earlier than expected. The procedure had gone swiftly without complications. All cancerous cells were removed so his mother-in-law required no further treatment, contrary to what the doctors had anticipated. Though things had gone well, Jim had feelings of anger and betrayal toward Ron because the surgery had not been averted. He wanted to lash out, verbalizing his animosity towards us. Then, something beyond his control happened. Right in the waiting room, the most amazing sense of peace came over him. Jim's anger melted away and no matter how hard he tried, he could no longer muster negative thoughts toward Ron.

Jim went on to tell us how his mother-in-law's recovery was supernaturally fast. As Thanksgiving arrived, she hosted the family dinner as usual. By Christmas, her energy returned as if she'd never had cancer nor undergone surgery. God restored her health completely, just not in the way we had hoped. The family praised the Lord, counting their blessings as never before.

We questioned: Could the Lord have already removed the cancer, accounting for the expedited surgery? Or, in the heavenly realm, was Ron seeing the end result?

In either case, Ron and I praised God for healing the woman *and* for intervening on our behalf! The Lord intercepted those curses headed our way. The power of our words and thoughts go forth to bless or to curse. "Death and life are in the power of the tongue . . ." (Proverbs 18:21). Choose life!

CHAPTER NINE

DIVINE REALIGNMENT

By Rachel Monahan

In May, 2003, I was given the opportunity to accompany my daughter, Nila, on a trip to Kansas. She was on schedule to attend a training workshop for her job as a Christian Radio Underwriter. I was excited to go, since I was not working at the time. Nila and I had always been close, and it would be a chance for much needed "girl time" as we drove together for two days.

As we settled into our trip, I noticed that I began to feel uncomfortable in my movements. When we stopped along the way for bathroom breaks, my joints ached as I got in and out of the van. We had taken the radio station's vehicle, which was a well-worn van with bucket seats. To add to my discomfort, the next day I could barely move without pain radiating from my hips and legs.

By the time we arrived at our destination, I could hardly lift myself out to the curb. The simple act of taking a step caused searing, almost unbearable pain. As an otherwise healthy and youthful "fifty-something," I was wondering, "What is happening to me?"

To make matters worse, the hotel's elevator was out of service. I had to drag myself up two flights of stairs, trying to remain positive, even as my body screamed out for relief from this awful torment. Instead of enjoying the quaint, beautiful room, I only wanted to lie down so I could feel better.

Nila attended her meetings, worrying all the while about leaving me alone to suffer in a strange place. As the time for departure drew near, I dreaded the drive back, wondering if I could possibly make it all that way with pain radiating from every inch of my body. In a matter of days, I had suddenly become like a sick old woman. I was very discouraged, but tried to be cheerful for my daughter's sake.

Nila appeared to remain positive in the face of my fears. However, without telling me, she had made the decision to drive all night to get me back home, praying for God's mercy and strength for us both. She told me later that she was terrified that I would die before she could return me safely home. I was that bad off. She felt in her heart that she had to get me home so that friends could come and lay hands on me in prayer, so I would be restored.

So in the wee hours of the morning, we arrived home, exhausted but relieved to be in familiar surroundings. By then I was almost completely paralyzed. My daughter had to carry me into the house and undress me for bed as I could not do anything for myself. We both prayed throughout the miserable and sleepless night.

The next morning, Nila called Christian friends to come to my home for prayer. A few minutes later, Debbie Reed called to ask if she could bring Ron and Glenda Pettey, a couple who walked in the ministry of healing and were eager to pray with anyone needing to be healed.

I had never met Ron and Glenda, but was so grateful that I begged her to please bring them as soon as possible. Nila helped me dress and brushed my hair so that I would look presentable, especially since I had spent the previous night in excruciating pain and fear. I knew I looked a fright!

After a brief introduction and hello, Ron stood back and looked purposefully at my body. I knew something was happening, but what? He said, "Please forgive me, but by looking, the Lord shows me what is going on inside the body, and then I pray accordingly." Glenda explained that the Lord shows Ron the physical problem through "X-ray" vision! I was astonished! At that point, I did not care how the Lord healed me, only that He would!

Ron was obviously concentrating hard, as he gently spoke. He explained that with my permission, Glenda would place her hand on my lower spine area, and he would place his hand on top of hers. They then anointed me with oil, laid hands on me and prayed to the Father to realign my spine. When they finished praying, they removed their hands and my pain was instantly gone! I was shocked, I could barely speak! It was the most wonderful feeling!

Next, Ron stepped back and looked at my body again. The Lord showed him that my hips were misaligned alongside my spine. He asked Nila to help him in praying for my hips. She did, and I felt even better!

A third time, Ron looked and felt the Lord showing him a blockage in my blood vessels on my right side. Again he prayed, this time for the blockage to be removed, and commanded my body to line up correctly. Immediately, I felt another change inside my body and realized that I actually felt really good for the first time in over a week!

Dazzled by the healing in my body and overwhelmed with thanksgiving, I joined my daughter and these faithful friends in praising God. I had joy, unspeakable joy, overflowing in my heart with the Lord's personal confirmation of His great love for me. I was totally healed!

The next day was Sunday and I went to church, eager to share with others what the Lord had done for me! I stood during the service and told of God's wonderful grace in healing my body. The congregation was overjoyed to hear it all! But in the midst of my excitement in sharing with my friends what had happened, the pain tried to come back. I silently forbade it. I stood firmly on God's promise of healing and refused any thought of allowing the pain to return.

The pain was persistent, flitting in and out of my body for about a week, but I would not accept it. I said over and over, aloud, "I am healed by the stripes of Jesus!" By the week's end, the evil pain had disappeared for good. Now, thirteen years later, I remain pain-free. I praise God for His marvelous love and care and shout, "Thank you, Jesus!"

CHAPTER TEN

GOD SEES YOUR HEART

Ron was receiving disability benefits because of the traumatic effects from his brain surgeries, though he appeared healthy. When people asked what he did for a livelihood, he was hard-pressed for an answer. As his supernatural gift of healing progressed, a friend joked that Ron could say he was "the Physician's assistant!" To name a specialty in the medical field, Ron would likely put the heart at the top of his list.

Ron's first vision was that of a heart. He frequently saw the heart's intricate workings. The Lord pinpointed the troublesome area. For example, Ron would see a heart valve off-beat or sticking. We asked the Lord for specific words to pray—God gave us the simple vocabulary and fixed the valve.

One year, Ron himself underwent medical heart tests. I was allowed to sit in on the echocardiogram and watch the large monitor showing Ron's heart rhythm and valve function. With the audio speaker turned up, the nurse positioned the screen for Ron to see. He affirmed, "That's exactly what I see when I pray for people's hearts!"

Hearts have many facets and healing takes many directions. Attending a beautiful wedding, Ron privately mentioned to me that he noticed that the bride carried an old wound—a broken heart. The outdoor wedding, complete with a lavish buffet and a live band, concealed that anything was amiss. "Ron, you can *see* that her heart is broken? How does this look?" I asked.

"Glenda, I can't really describe it—it's a jagged line fragmenting her heart. In fact, I believe every young woman here has a broken heart as well!"

"Ron, how can we pray for the bride and all her friends?" I whispered. "We know God can intervene!" We quietly asked Father God to draw these young women to Himself and meet their emotional needs as only He can. "Heal their broken hearts!"

During the prayer line in a church, Jana, an attractive woman in her early thirties, approached us, supported by a friend on each side. Ron immediately asked, "Why am I seeing two hearts? This is very disturbing!" Instantly the friends chimed in that Jana's mother was currently hospitalized for an uncertain illness, demanding her daughter be at her side. Jana, weary from spending days at the hospital, admitted her mother was undermining her second marriage, as she had done with the first.

"That's why I'm seeing two hearts!" Ron said. "You have been double-minded in your allegiance to your husband. You love your mother, but you have also made a vow to honor your marriage."

Ron prayed, "Father, I ask You to show Jana *Your* heart in this matter. Reveal Your Will in her life—how she is to care for her mother while cleaving to her husband, as they have become one in You."

Jana agreed. She prayed aloud, repenting of her conflicted heart as her friends upheld her. Visible to all of us, Jana's tears signaled the release of the burdens she had carried for so long.

In that moment Ron spoke, "You have only one heart now . . . I just saw them come together as one! Hallelujah!"

Keep your heart with all diligence,
for out of it spring the issues of life.

—Proverbs 4:23

Peace I leave with you. My peace I give to you;
not as the world gives do I give to you. Let not
your heart be troubled, neither let it be afraid.

—John 14:27

And the peace of God, which transcends
all understanding, will guard your hearts
and your minds in Christ Jesus.

—Philippians 4:7

CHAPTER ELEVEN

THE KINGDOM CONNECTION

I n the spring of 2004, Ron gave an interview at a local Christian radio station. Upon hearing Ron speak, a member of a small local church called her pastor, insisting that he contact us. The next day, Pastor Larry Poret invited us to his home, where his living room was packed with members wanting to hear a firsthand account of Heaven. Speaking engagements at his church and other venues followed. This was the beginning of our lifelong friendship with Larry. Larry shares the details:

> The air of expectancy in my house the night we had invited the Petteys was unlike anything I had ever experienced. Every seat in my living room was taken and the floor space, as well. We sang for thirty minutes while waiting for the couple to arrive. We

were amazed with Ron's account of his trip to Heaven, but even more with his humility and demeanor. Everyone in the group asked for prayer. Ron took one man aside to speak quietly to him, discerning the need for privacy. "Come into my office," he joked!

The healing I had that night was profound. Little did anyone know that painful bunions on both my feet had returned months after surgery. Ron prayed for my feet and they were instantly healed and have not bothered me since!

On separate occasions, my son and brother were also healed, both avoiding future surgeries—to the amazement of their individual doctors.

Throughout the years that I have known Ron and the times I've heard him speak, I believe that *restoring hope* was the greater result of sharing his testimony. Ron always exuded compassion as he tirelessly focused on the needs of others. Faith, Hope and Love were the heart of his message.

At our invitation, Larry soon connected with our prayer group, The Order of St. Luke. Eventually, Larry transitioned back into the workforce, planning to own a restaurant. On one Tuesday night at the OSL meeting, Amy, who was hoping to sell a small restaurant, met Larry. Offered an almost-too-good-to-be-true deal, Larry bought the barbecue diner in Amy's hometown. The restaurant's maintenance man, Bruce Miller, stayed on to work with Larry. Soon, Larry was back in town, bringing Bruce to the OSL meeting. Bruce had family ties to a Christian camp near Hot Springs, Arkansas.

In a couple of weeks, the camp's owner invited us to any and all of the scheduled camp meetings.

We were given free rein on the morning we were on the program. A distinguished and well-dressed couple sat in the audience, chiming in on our talk. Afterwards, the couple insisted on taking us to their home nearby to pray for their grown daughter via phone. We soon discovered that we had met Clement and Frances Faye Humbard, celebrities in their own right!

The Humbard Family, led by brothers Rex and Clement, were trailblazers of nondenominational tent revivals across America from the late '40s to the mid-'60s and pioneers of televised services. By 1965, Rex put down ministry roots just outside Akron, Ohio, where he built the spectacular Church of Tomorrow. Clement pastored near Youngstown, Ohio, and continued with worldwide ministry as well. Frances joined him in 1982.

Quickly, Clement and Frances Faye Humbard became our mentors and friends. A month after we met them we were back in Arkansas. Through their initiative, ministry doors were flung open for us with invitations to return. Clement loved introducing Ron at each event. Frances invited guests for lunch or dinner, or just asked them to drop in for prayer and coffee. She took every opportunity to connect us to those who needed prayer and encouragement.

Clement entertained us with his endless array of fascinating stories. He and Frances filled a void in our lives with their mature, wise counsel and practical advice. Even though I took notes, the personal time we spent with them was simply too brief.

Once, I arrived in Arkansas with a new hairstyle that needed help. Frances took me to her stylist at the first break in our schedule. *Friends don't let friends look bad!* (Smile!)

Clement and Frances temporarily relocated to Florida by Christmas in 2008. The Lord strategically placed them there to connect with us on our first major outing in January 2009. Frances' gift of hospitality and arranging ministry appointments for us continued in Florida, just as it had in Arkansas.

Frances recalls several pivotal moments we had together:

> Clement and I were with Ron and Glenda Pettey on occasions when we all witnessed the supernatural power of God at work. Once we were eating breakfast with a couple who were local pastors. They apologized for bringing their infant granddaughter along, as her babysitter had canceled. When the child began to cry, the grandmother could not quiet her. Ron looked at the infant and asked, "Has this child had a medical check-up that would indicate a problem with her heart?" We stopped eating. All eyes were focused on the grandparents. Ron looked at Glenda and said softly, "I have seen this condition before when there were Native American bloodlines. It was a curse resulting from rituals using an animal heart." Ron looked at the grandmother and asked, "Do you have Native American ancestors?" No one moved except the infant who continued to cry. Then the grandmother answered, "Yes." After a brief prayer of "identification repentance" for the sins of the forefathers, Ron prayed for the heart to be healed. The child was quickly soothed and stopped crying.

Another time we asked Ron to help our friend, a Hispanic pastor who suffered with severe allergies. Ron reached over and brushed the Spirit of Self-Pity off his shoulder, commanding it to leave. The pastor humbled himself and asked Ron, "What do you think this is about?" Ron looked him in the eye and said, "You are very busy with the ministry. At times you feel that you are the only one doing anything and that you are carrying the whole workload." The pastor chuckled and acknowledged this truth. The spirit left. No one was surprised that his chronic allergies dramatically improved.

On my last visit with Ron, we sat in the hotel lobby waiting for Glenda. Ron began explaining that what he was seeing in the spirit realm pertained to me. "Jesus is standing before us," Ron said, "and He wants to give you a gift—one that I don't see you have need of. He wants to give you 'more confidence'." Like children, we both chuckled. But God knows best. And Ron had learned to say what he was seeing and hearing in the Spirit Realm. God knows it will surely take "more confidence" for all of us to rest in Him as He finishes His work through us.

For the first year or so after Clement's death, prophets would call and say that Clement had appeared to them with an assignment or a word. I asked Ron if he had encountered such a visitation from Clement. Ron stopped for a moment, gave a little chuckle and said, "Yes. He came to me and said, 'Ron, at these meetings when you are praying for the masses, remember to pray for the children.'" Glenda looked at him in amazement, hearing this for the first time.

Ron was not a man-pleaser. He was always conscious of Christ's presence. He had such reverence . . . like the little flowers he had seen in Heaven that bowed at the sight of the Savior. Ron maintained a reverent attitude in the natural and in the spirit, so he was always in tune with the heavenlies, bowing before the King of Glory.

CHAPTER TWELVE

WHERE'S MY NURSE?

At the 2005 OSL Conference held at St. Cyprian's Episcopal Church in Lufkin, Ron and I served as a prayer team, available at the close of each session. The following week, Mignon Murrell, who had attended the conference, called us wanting to schedule a private prayer session. Her two-hour drive from Houston back to Lufkin was not a concern.

The next week we met Mignon at our church prayer room. We would soon discover that God was introducing us to our next best friend! As we heard her health concerns and prayed for her that day, Mignon heard the Lord say, "I'm connecting you!" Though a little surprised, she said, "Okay, Lord."

In two weeks, another OSL Conference that we had planned to attend was being held in Mignon's area of Houston. She graciously offered us her guest room. I was stunned when Ron agreed, "Sure . . . great. Why not?"

Mignon and her husband, Bill, were accomplished musicians, as I could see from posters of past gigs on display. Among their many talents, Bill played acoustic guitar, Mignon sang, together they wrote, arranged and recorded music for themselves and others. Right away we also discovered that Mignon could entertain! Her quick wit and hilarious one-liners gave us belly laughs that were long overdue—a release from the gravity of our ministry. What good therapy to laugh!

A month or so afterward, Mignon insisted that we needed a website. We were embarrassingly behind in the world of technology! She moved into our house for a few days and worked tirelessly to create not only a beautiful format but all the content as well. As a result of the website, we were soon receiving calls and invitations to speak.

Pastor Larry and Vickie Phillips were among the first to call, asking us to come to their tent meeting in Orange, Texas. They had erected a large tent right beside their church building. Vickie had envisioned the tent sending a welcoming message to the community, liberating the gospel from behind the four walls! It worked, as people filled the tent with excitement and anticipation of what the Holy Spirit would do!

Any speaker knows what a difference the mood of an audience can make. This crowd was super-charged! Ron was more animated than usual, enjoying every minute to brag on the goodness of God. Everyone took a turn in the prayer line. Pastor Larry realized that several of his members needed private quality time with Ron, so he begged us to stay over another night. He roughed out an appointment schedule in thirty-minute intervals, for Ron to have individual ministry at the church the next day.

Mid-morning, Yvette came in, pale and weak. She'd spent the long weekend in the local hospital with pain in her chest and extreme weakness in her left arm. As soon as she sat down in front of us, Ron "saw" a tiny blood clot in the back of her heart, so small, he called it a *BB*. Ron clearly heard the Lord say for Yvette to walk the perimeter of the large room. Though weak, she got up and walked. When she returned to her seat, Ron peered again and noticed some improvement. The Lord instructed her to walk again, this time three laps around the room. When she returned this time, she was visibly changed. The pain and weakness had left her chest and arm. Her strength and energy fully returned! We praised the Lord!

Back in Lufkin at our OSL prayer group, we shared Yvette's story. Our friend Brigitte, a nurse with extensive ER experience, listened intently and began to explain what Ron had seen. The EKG at the hospital had not picked up the tiny BB on the back side of Yvette's heart. It was exactly in the blind spot of the machine. Brigitte was appalled that the hospital had released Yvette, feeling that the girl was literally having a heart attack! After that night, as Ron prayed for someone and saw an internal part he didn't recognize, he would cry, "Where's my nurse?" Brigitte would often be on the scene and medically explain what Ron was seeing. Afterward, on outings across the country, people heard Ron call for the nurse!

The Lord had more plans for our friend, Brigitte. In addition to nursing skills, Brigitte was also handy with computers. In 2008, with our email overflowing with prayer requests and book orders following an interview with Sid Roth, Brigitte stepped in to help. Then, during our 2009-2010 years of travel, Brigitte worked as my right-hand woman, anchoring R&G Ministries (Ron & Glenda) while we traveled! More significantly, the Lord promoted Brigitte to intercession. The Lord gave her dreams and directions of how to pray for people, specifically us! We cannot underestimate the value of intercessors lifting us up, especially with the spiritual radar that God gives them!

Brigitte recalls the first time we met and our ongoing friendship:

> I met Ron and Glenda Pettey at church in the early 2000s. My first encounter with Ron's praying for me was one Sunday after I had been working a long week as a nurse in Houston. I had been on my feet for most of my twelve-hour shifts and I had great pain in my lower back—a chronic condition I had had for years. I was new to this church and new to living as a Christian. I didn't really know what to expect but I was determined to have someone pray for me. I noticed that the pastor had directed several people to come to the front as prayer teams, and one of the teams was Ron and Glenda. I chose them to pray for me.
>
> When I told them of my health concern, Ron asked my permission for Glenda to run her hand over my entire spine before they focused on my lower back. Ron "saw" a large weight—I wondered what on earth he was "seeing," but I don't recall asking him to explain. He told Glenda that they both needed to "pull" something from my back. I thought, "Okay, this is interesting!" When they pantomimed with their hands and lifted off something invisible, I felt the most incredible thing—the weight from my back was gone! I even jumped forward, almost frightened by the sensation. The pain left

my body at that moment. This was my first encounter with the supernatural—the first of many more to come.

A few years later, I renewed my acquaintance with Ron and Glenda when I joined their OSL prayer group. As a nurse, I was inspired by the healing stories of Jesus. I was trained in the scientific world of medicine and surgery, but I was intrigued to learn of healing through prayer. As I attended the meetings and listened to Ron expound on seeing angels, I had to stretch to believe him. However, over time I came to realize that Ron was indeed a unique and gifted man of God. He was plain spoken—he was not a boisterous man, but humble and genuine. While he may have struggled to recall routine details from everyday life, his Heaven experience was fresh in his mind, as if it had just happened. I rationalized that God may have limited Ron to keep him humble—to prevent him from becoming haughty. Ron often asked, "Why did God give me this gift?" My husband replied, "Ron, God knew He could trust you."

I became even closer to the couple as I helped Glenda care for Ron during his last eighteen months of life. Ron never complained, in fact, he was typically cracking jokes, even when I knew he wasn't feeling well. He was always trying to lighten the heaviness of the situation and make people laugh. I often found myself wanting to sit and listen to him tell stories. Glenda would help fill in the blanks for Ron if he left out a detail along the way. His twinkling blue eyes and giant smile and sense of humor were his trademarks.

Quite a few times when I arrived at their home, Ron would be on a telephone prayer call. Glenda would introduce me into the conversation, put the speaker on and direct me to join in counseling and praying for the person. Rarely, if ever, did the caller know Ron's own physical struggle.

I found myself asking God, "Why isn't this man healed?" I prayed for him on a regular basis, even when he appeared to be at the brink of death. I saw him recover but never to his full vitality. God knew Ron's struggle and the length of his days; I, on the other hand, questioned why Ron wasn't fully healed. This was a mystery I was not meant to know.

A week or so after Ron's passing, the Lord gave me a supernatural, quick glimpse of him. In a flash, I saw Ron so clearly in his heavenly state, quite a bit younger, with longer, lighter brown hair but sporting his familiar, warm smile. Ron was sitting under what looked like a willow tree, enjoying an apple-sized red berry in his hand, something between a raspberry and a strawberry. I am amazed at how that brief moment seemed like ten minutes as I observed all the details! What a contrast from earth to Heaven! This vision, after having to say goodbye too soon to my dear friend, was God's gift to me!

CHAPTER THIRTEEN

SAVED FROM A GENERATIONAL STRONGHOLD

By Steven J. Lumbley

On June 4, 2007, I was being deployed to Iraq for my second tour of duty. I knew something was wrong with me. My strength was dwindling. I had started coughing up blood while I was working out, and I could not stop gagging in the mornings. I could literally feel something inside me, eating my life away.

I was living for myself, smoking packs of cigarettes a day and drinking excessively. Yet despite my sinful and unhealthy lifestyle, the Lord had not given up on me. He began to give me meaningful dreams that He was a supernaturally healing God. The closer I got to my departure date, the more I started to feel something was really wrong, deep inside me. I was struggling with numerous problems.

To top it off, my grandmother's cancer had returned and she was sick in bed. Though her cancer had been in remission for twelve or thirteen years, she could never put cigarettes down for good. In 2005, X-rays showed tumors in her lungs. My grandmother's father was a smoker and my grandfather on my dad's side was also addicted to tobacco. I, too, was hooked on cigarettes and could not go more than five minutes without a smoke. I had smoked, off and on, since 2001 and before that I had snuck Virginia Slims from my grandmother. I remember thinking how cool she looked when she smoked, and how the lady on the carton with the fancy hat pulled over her eyes seemed so attractive to me.

I had met Ron and Glenda Pettey a couple of years earlier and knew how the Lord was using them in amazing ways. The closer my deployment came, the more I struggled to call the Petteys, fearful of what Ron might see. On June 2 I finally worked up enough nerve to call and ask that they pray for me. The next day, they came to my mother's house and we were to meet in an empty back room for prayer. I was nervous when I saw them pull up. I started to hug Ron but I just shook his hand instead. Later, I found out that the Lord cautioned Ron against hugging me because of what he was already seeing.

We gathered in the back room and arranged our chairs in a circle. In the quiet room, with privacy from the rest of the family, I thanked Ron and Glenda for coming and informed them of my desperate situation. I confessed, "I need help with my smoking problem." Ron was directly across from me and I'll never forget his face. He was looking deeply at my chest and causing me to feel uncomfortable. Ron had this look about him that suggests he is seeing more than we know. Then, after a few seconds of his staring at my chest, he informed me that I had cancer! I was more scared at that moment than I had been at any point in my whole life! I almost got sick right there. Ron pointed, "Steven, it's right there. I can see it, and it's all over you." I can't put into words what was going through my mind. Ron could really see what was inside of me and described it as imps or little demons running amok. He asked me how long I had been smoking and I told him, "Off and on for about six years." Ron replied, "Steven, you have the lungs of someone who has been smoking for twenty years!"

Ron stood up to anoint my head with oil. I just remember praying and asking God to forgive me for what I had done to my body. My heart was racing, but when Ron touched my chest, the beats returned to normal. During the prayer time Ron told me, "Steven, it [cancer] has literally eaten through the left side of your lung."

My mother joined us and prayed, repenting for me and all of our family who had smoked, asking the Lord to break the generational stronghold that tobacco has had on our family. Ron asked me once more, "Steven, how long did you say you had been smoking?" He just couldn't believe the dire condition of my lungs. Ron directed my mother to put her hand on my chest as we continued to pray. I felt a surge of healing throughout my chest, the power of the Holy Spirit! Simultaneously, Ron shouted, "It's gone!"

What a celebration! When we finally caught our breath from the miracle we had witnessed, I had one more request. I asked my wife and mother to leave the room for Ron to pray for another concern, an infection that was known only to me. As we prayed, Ron simply announced, "It's not there anymore, it's gone!" To this day it's never appeared again.

I was finally able to hug Ron like I wanted to do when I first saw him. As we were leaving the room, Ron specifically told me to share my experience with my brothers with whom I was deploying, and to encourage them to stop smoking.

During the deployment, I can tell you that many of the men close to me either quit smoking for good or were able to try. After the Lord had touched and healed my lungs, Glenda prayed that I would have favor in my chain of command. That prophetic word became true during my deployment as I was delegated duties over men with more rank and experience. At times, I had as many as fifty-five men and some four hundred detainees for whom I was responsible. I was constantly in the favor of my commander and 1st Sergeant, and basically a favorite among most of the men with whom I served.

Since that day that the Lord used Ron and Glenda as instruments of healing through the glory of our Lord and Savior, my life has been changed. Many people have heard my testimony, and if they haven't given their lives to the Lord already, then I pray that they will. The Lord chastens those He loves, and He loves all. He wishes none to perish but for all to come to Him so He can unlock His blessings in their lives. Some people are so hard-headed and so wasted away in sin, only a miracle can get them on track with the Lord. I had hit rock bottom and had nowhere else to turn. Now, through the power of prayer, devotion and fasting, I am blessed in my marriage and the new job God has given me with the church I attend. I encourage you to step out and believe the supernatural powers of our Lord and give all Glory to Him!

CHAPTER FOURTEEN

"IT'S SUPERNATURAL!"

In the spring of 2008, we accepted a wonderful invitation to spend a week in Junction, Texas, a scenic town nestled in the West Texas hill country. We'd met our hosts, Pastors Gary and Elaine Niesmier, at a conference earlier.

The Niesmiers clearly heard and obeyed the Lord's direction to set up ministry meetings, backyard barbeques and one-on-ones with a diverse cross section of the town's population. Our days were filled with divine appointments and southern hospitality! We felt the Lord's anointing in the guest house upon our arrival, and His spirit of favor throughout our stay.

One of Elaine's sweet friends, Ann, had emotional inner healing from her addictions of overeating and buying lottery tickets. We learned that the two destructive habits were related by a "fear of lack!" Like a squirrel burying nuts for the winter, she had been storing food while dreading financial shortage. With new freedom from these strangleholds, Ann refocused on her purpose in life, to pray and intercede for others. She became a serious intercessor for us.

By the end of our week, on our way out of Junction, Elaine asked to meet us at the home of another pastor and his wife. Elaine had just learned of the man's illness which had kept him bedridden for a week. The three of us met and prayed with the couple for a short time. When we left the house, Ron and I continued our visit with Elaine out on the lawn. While we were chatting, the couple came out, dressed and smiling, on their way to a restaurant for lunch!

The next week when we were back at home, a phone call came from Sid Roth's ministry inviting us to be guests on his radio and TV programs, "It's Supernatural!" We learned that a family we had prayed with months earlier had sent our book to Sid. With hundreds of submissions, the Lord allowed ours to float to the top and be discovered by Sid's team. The staff immediately agreed that our story should be selected, along with the reenactments from the Actors' Guild in California.

Over the past sixteen years that we had been sharing our story with individuals and small groups, the Lord had been grooming us as well as humbling us all along the way. Now He was trusting us with a *big stage*! We were given a phone interview appointment which would be recorded for a five-segment radio spot, and had travel arrangements made for us to tape an episode of "It's Supernatural!" at the INSP studio in Charlotte, North Carolina.

Meeting Sid Roth was quite a trip! After the lengthy long-distance phone interview, Sid asked, "Ron, can you see my guardian angel?" Ron surprised me when he answered, "Yes!" He began to describe the angel. I had to interject, "Ron, you're describing Sid!" As Ron had experienced, guardian angels resemble the person they are assigned to guard, and Sid was no exception.

Just ten days after the phone interview, we flew to Charlotte to meet in person with Sid Roth, his staff and several other guests for the taping. What a glorious experience! The first night following dinner at the hotel, Sid asked Ron to pray for him. Sid was amazed at the accuracy with which the Lord revealed and healed his physical and spiritual condition that was shown to Ron.

At the end of the taping session the next day, we were delighted to meet two special ladies, the intercessors, who sat in the studio to pray throughout the day. The three-day event was covered in prayer, averting weather and flight-related dilemmas and challenges of all sorts.

Our program was scheduled to air Thanksgiving week and again during December, 2008. We were warned that this exposure would change our lives! God, help us!

(From top to bottom:) Sid reviewing his notes.
On the set of "It's Supernatural!"
We Love the intercessors!

CHAPTER FIFTEEN

ON THE ROAD
AND IN THE AIR

After our episode of "It's Supernatural!" aired, emails flooded in, along with phone calls as Ron chose to keep our home phone number listed for the public. By early January, ministry trips were on our calendar. The year 2009 would be quite busy: ministry trips to eight states, weddings for two of our children, the birth of our first grandchild and Ron's mother's home-going.

Beyond the church services and ministry time were divine appointments. In Orlando, Florida, we ministered at House of Hope, a beautiful safe haven—a place of healing for troubled teens, founded in 1985 by Sara Trollinger. We were invited to stay in one of the guest houses for several days while we spoke at their chapel and ministered to the teenagers and their parents. Ms. Trollinger graciously allowed visitors who had followed our itinerary to attend the meetings inside the private gated campus.

We just so happened to be at House of Hope during its annual board meeting which included supporters from all over the country. Ben and Brenda Peters, former guests of "It's Supernatural!" were among those present. Brenda was known for her prophetic gifting, and Ben was recognized as a writer and teacher.

The Peters invited us to join them in the greater Chicago area later that spring where they had a broad base of ministry. We joined them there, and at the first event, several young people asked Ron to pray that they themselves would have supernatural X-ray vision—a difficult prayer request for us to consider. Knowing the trauma Ron had experienced to arrive at this point in his life, we searched for an answer. We prayed with confidence that Father God would arm each one with unique skills and provisions according to His perfect and foreordained will. If that involved supernatural vision, the Lord would give it freely. God would not withhold any good gift from His beloved—His desire is for everyone to fulfill his unique destiny.

The next day, Ben Peters took us to an outlying town where a church met in a business strip-center. The wife pastored the lively congregation while her husband, a dentist, officed next door. Their Sunday routine was to serve a potluck lunch after the service as the members came from all directions of the metroplex. Crock pots with wonderful aromas lined a counter.

The pastor and her dentist husband were last in the prayer line that day. When we were able to visit, the husband admitted to us that the Lord had given him X-ray vision when examining his patients. He could "see" cavities and the health of his patients' teeth—he knew ahead of the physical X-rays what the outcome would be. He rarely, if ever, told anyone of this unusual gift, especially since he wanted to keep his dental practice intact! The regular X-rays always confirmed what he expected. What a joy to fellowship with these believers! God loved to surprise us!

Through email, we met Steven Collar, a man who had survived a horrific trampoline accident requiring major surgeries. Yet, like Ron, the Lord had given him supernatural abilities. During his lengthy recovery, Steven and his family had relocated to Redding, California, to attend Pastor Bill Johnson's ministry school at Bethel Church. With an invitation from friends to come to Redding, we made the trip in March to meet Steven. What a treat for the two men to stand face-to-face, both with the strange gift of X-ray vision! Ron could see Steven's steel rods supporting both sides of his neck while Steven could watch the shunt carrying spinal fluid in Ron's head! With that awkward introduction out of the way, we had great fellowship, which developed into an ongoing friendship. Steven asked us to his Monday night home group meeting to be introduced to the leader, veteran minister celebrity Ray Mossholder. Ray, in turn, took us to the private weekly pastors' meeting where we received a warm welcome from Bill Johnson, and an extended prayer time with Bill and the dozen gathered in that "upper room." Joaquin Evans, leader of the Bethel Healing Room where creative miracles were common, asked the Lord to increase the healing anointing for Ron. God alone knows the significance of that prayer, as we continued to see a tangible display of His touch everywhere we went.

By mid-summer 2009, we received a written note with a book order from Allison Restagno in Canada. After she had read our book, she emailed her comments and impressions of our story. Then, via phone calls, Allison explained the Lord's mandate for her to compile a book of fifty miraculous testimonies: she was certain that ours was to be on the list. I would need to write a fresh synopsis of our life story for a chapter in her book. Not until two other ministries asked for the same thing (one for an online blog and another for a magazine in print) did I begin to take the assignment seriously. So, in our busy schedule, I submitted what would become Chapter 21 in Allison Restagno's *Modern Day Miracles*.

By the fall of 2010, Allison had a publisher, and her book was ready to print. We made plans to join other contributors in celebrating the pre-launch of the book in Canada. Had Frances Humbard not prepared us to *stretch* for adventures such as this, I doubt we could have done it! I booked our flights, rental car and hotel room, with no clear financial sponsor. Frances had instilled in us that we were to go as the Lord leads, trusting Him to make the way.

As the time of the event approached, the Lord instructed Allison to take an offering on our behalf to help defray expenses. We were traveling farther and at greater expense than any of the other guests. On the night of the banquet, she graciously explained her mission to financially assist us. She passed a basket which friends filled with American and Canadian dollars. What a testimony when the cash exactly matched the hotel bill, half in one currency and half in the other!

The first week of December, 2010, was a flurry of activity. We flew into Buffalo, New York, rented a car and drove to Burlington, Ontario, the hub for the week's itinerary.

Allison's firsthand account follows:

> As I watched "It's Supernatural!" in December 2008, I felt an immediate connection to the Petteys. I found their website and sent them a note with a money order, requesting their book. When the book

arrived, I could not put it down. The Lord showed me that their ministry was anointed and full of the Holy Spirit's power. I knew then that Ron and Glenda were an exact match for testimony contributors in my book, *Modern Day Miracles*.

After several emails, I was warmly welcomed over the phone into their home on a weekly, and even sometimes, on a daily basis. We soon learned that we had much in common in the spiritual realm.

When Ron and Glenda came up for the week in December 2010, I coordinated several events for the contributors to meet and greet. It was a delightful tour of Niagara-On-The-Lake, Niagara Falls, Ontario, along with individual fellowship times, culminating with a catered banquet at a quiet little church. Our initial meeting at a luncheon at my house had been so special to me.

Ron walked through my front door and exclaimed that angels were positioned there and elsewhere in my home. I was thrilled to hear this, though not surprised, as I felt they were assigned to protect me from the intense warfare I encountered while compiling the book. Ron went on to reveal more of what the Lord was telling him, saying that I would climb up all levels of ministry, but that it would occur naturally for me—the Lord would do this for His Divine purpose. With vivid excitement, he added that I had no idea of the great names in ministry who would be coming to my home to sit at my dining room table. As of 2016, that has already happened on several occasions, all for God's glory!

The Petteys gave an extensive radio interview and taped an interview with "100 Huntley Street," the longest running daily television show in Canada, along with ministering to individuals during their week here. When their interview with Moira Brown aired the following week, the Petteys received prayer requests and book orders from every province in Canada. The program remains on the station's website and on YouTube.

At the beautiful Crossroads Centre complex in Burlington, Ontario, our Monday morning schedule with "100 Huntley Street" was a tight fit to make our return flight in Buffalo, New York, connecting back to Texas. An earlier taping ran overtime, causing ours to begin much later than planned. While in the green room, I was watching the clock! Then we met our TV host, Moira Brown, who was warm and gracious and well prepared for our interview. Our taping ticked off quickly. Then, with the interview over, cameras off, Moira began a wonderful conversation. We were joined by host, Jim Cantelon, and a couple of cameramen. *This* is the conversation that should have been aired! Now, it was as if time stood still!

Allison, with prophetic accuracy at her home in another town, sensed our predicament. She literally saw us sitting and chatting with no thought of time slipping away. She called a friend at the station for help. That friend ran from her office across the complex, burst into the studio, shouting, "Get up and get moving . . . you're about to miss your flight!" The TV staff helped us gather our belongings and get to our car. As we drove out a few miles, the weather conditions suddenly made the roadway treacherous with ice and sleet. The 100-plus kilometer drive on Queen Elizabeth Way would take twice the time today! Allison called our cell phone, warning me to keep a safe distance from the car ahead. Again, she was seeing the situation accurately. I had already tried to pass that car and found the ice so thick that changing lanes was impossible. I did slow down! By God's grace, we were expedited through customs and managed to take the correct exits to arrive at the airport. The rental car agent didn't question me when I demanded that she get in the driver's seat and deliver us to our gate. We boarded in split-second timing before the flight departed!

Allison continues:

> From our meeting in 2010 to Ron's home-going, I had such joy in sharing the visions that the Lord had given me with Ron. On one occasion, I described in detail a scene of a mansion in Heaven. Ron exclaimed, "I've been there! Yes, I know that place!" Glenda would lovingly scold him and teasingly say, "Ron, why haven't you told me this? Yet, I find out now, after all of these years!" He would laugh, and she would, too. It was such a joy to see them so in love with each other and so in love with the Lord, as they enjoyed doing His Kingdom work!
>
> Throughout the year before Ron's home-going, he encouraged me to publish a second book, a compilation of forty testimonies of amazing salvation experiences. *Modern Day Salvation Encounters* is now in its final stages of publication.

I believe that Ron is smiling in that "great cloud of witnesses" in Heaven and is most pleased with his wife's willingness and skill to write this book. Even now, I see him nodding, "Yes!" and waving a pen in his hand.

(From top to bottom:) Ron sharing the good news. Lollipop on her way to a Christmas event to share Christ with Santa and the elves. Radio Interview in Brantford, Ontario with Vicki Schliefer. On the "100 Huntley Street" set with the host Moira Brown.

CHAPTER SIXTEEN

A CONVERSATION WITH FRIENDS

Bob Walker: Ron was my dear friend and prayer partner. We worked together for many years before my move to Minnesota. I'll never forget the shock on our faces when the Lord healed Don, the attorney, right in front of our eyes! Ron and I watched his twisted leg straighten and lengthen, and then we saw him walk without his crutches! Later, after his doctor's visit, Don joyfully reported that he would not need further surgeries.

Another of my favorite times was when Ron and I were called to the hospital ER to pray for a lady who had suffered a massive heart attack. When we arrived, we prayed for her deadly low blood pressure to rise. Then, as we watched the monitors, her pressure gradually returned to normal. She opened her eyes, asked for pen and paper and wrote, "Unhook me from all this stuff!" The doctors were reluctant to do so, but she insisted. She immediately sat up and began to talk with no pain. She was released the next day, and even the doctors acknowledged that her recovery was a miracle. One of the housekeeping ladies saw what had happened that evening, so then we prayed for her, and she gave her heart and life to the Lord. When the patient's son and his wife arrived from another town, they saw their mother walking, joking and talking about God's love. They began to weep and rejoice! Ron and I had a glorious time leading them to the Lord. Wow! What a night!

Glenda: I remember that night! We spoke with her stepdaughter months later to hear that she remained in good health and in awe of God's love and healing.

Pam: I met you in 2001 as our mothers had become friends at their retirement complex. On one visit with my parents, we became better acquainted and Ron invited me to the OSL prayer group on Tuesday nights. It wasn't long before I observed and experienced firsthand Ron's unusual spiritual gift. I witnessed this gift at work many times, not only in prayer meetings but also just anywhere he happened to be. Ron prayed for my gum problem and my pain disappeared—immediately. Another time, he pointed out a highlighted area in my neck and asked to pray for it. My doctor had just reported that I had a clogged carotid artery, and later I would have test results of its clearing.

Robert: My wife, Phyllis, was at the church fish fry when Ron's memory returned in 1992. I first met Ron on a home-school outing in the fall of 1989. On a day trip out to a state park, I had arrived a little late and the nature hike had just started. Catching up to the group, I saw a new visitor just ahead of me. As I drew closer I could hear him telling a story. I began hearing bits and pieces of a narrative containing many strange and unusual events. I heard, " . . . And then I could see the angel standing in the corner of the room . . . and I saw myself lying on the table . . . and my good friend was leading the congregation in prayer for me . . . there was this bright light . . ." I must say, these sentence fragments immediately caught my attention! I wondered why all of these people weren't sitting and listening to this man speak. I still wonder about that. In time, I not only heard the whole story but also enjoyed the privilege of getting to know Ron and your entire family.

Phyllis: With the return of Ron's memory, we all hoped and prayed for continued healing so that he would eventually be completely healed in every way. When some maladies lingered, we were confused and bewildered. God was using Ron to pray for others, and in response to the prayers, God healed . . . but Ron was not totally healed. As I read and hear of the physical and spiritual healings, I am in awe. But as great as those are to me, a greater miracle is the sustaining grace of God in your lives for thirty-three years as you lived through multiple trials and setbacks. So many times you experienced a "new normal" when the latest health challenge required a different way of coping. The ten years of no short-term memory must have seemed like an eternity. The onset of diabetes mandated changes in lifestyle and in care-giving procedures. The symptoms of multiple sclerosis increased the demands on your patience and endurance and produced the strain of adapting to new equipment. The miracle in it all was that there was *no bitterness* toward God who, though He healed hundreds of others, He did not heal Ron. Your praise and worship just intensified. Was that not an awesome miracle?

Betty: I agree with you, Phyllis. My experience with Ron goes back to the mid-'90s when Ron and Glenda were just beginning to learn of a spirit-filled lifestyle like the disciples experienced in the New Testament. What a transition that was! The thought of spiritual gifts, such as a healing anointing, were foreign to Ron—much less that he would possess it! I remember one Sunday at church when Ron's vision into the spiritual realm became overwhelming to him. He had to leave the service to get away from the distractions. He was upset with the visual overload and was praying for the Lord to remove the *gift of supernatural sight,* when one of our friends intercepted him in the foyer. Paul convinced Ron that his gift was needed and that the Lord would help. Soon, someone else passed through the foyer and took advantage of Ron's being available to pray for him. In a few minutes, someone else showed up. In no time, Ron was back in his "element." Healing was happening and the recipients weren't being shy! Before the morning service ended, there were at least a dozen of us having quite a good time! My husband, Ray, was one healed that morning. Chest pain from his two stents cleared completely. He canceled his doctor's appointment the next day and hasn't been back since! The pastor, my brother Simon, was not bothered by this noisy interruption outside the sanctuary. He managed to finish his sermon and rejoice that God had another agenda that day, knowing that His ways are higher than ours!

Joe: I first met you at Bob Flournoy's Thursday night meeting. Right away, I invited you to speak to my college psychology class at the end of the semester during our chapter on "Death and Dying."

Glenda: Joe, can you believe that we were there every semester, including the summers, for nine years? You warned us not to preach, just to tell our story. We left clicking our heels every time—those were the very best times of our lives!

Joe: I loved watching the students' reactions. The vast majority were overwhelmed and you could see it in their faces—God is real—there is a Heaven! The day Ron spoke, no one left early and most remained to ask questions after the class had officially ended.

Coach Hester: I regularly listened to Sid Roth's program and when I heard you guys, I knew I had to order your book. What a surprise when I read you lived within driving distance from me! I called to set a time to come meet you. As a result, my wife Barbara and I began joining you every week at your church. I arranged a prayer session for my son, Lance, for Ron to pray for healing from his seizures. From that one meeting, Lance was healed. My granddaughter, Morgan, experienced a similar healing when Ron prayed for her, and it was confirmed by her EKG reports. Ron reported seeing five large angels surrounding Morgan, in addition to her guardian angel. One angel was wearing a lavish, expensive-looking robe that Ron was told represented "Morgan's compassionate heart." This vision was quite a comfort to all our family, because she would go through tumultuous teen years before coming to the end of a rebellious cycle and finding her purpose in Christ.

I coached at a high school a couple of hours away from Ron and Glenda, and I called them several times to pray for my colleagues. Ron directed me to hand my cell phone to them, right then, and pray. I was intrigued as I watched them voice a prayer and saw their countenances change. "How does Ron do this?" we wondered. Dave had immediate relief from intense joint pain, and the Lord corrected John's dangerously clogged artery, right there on the ball field.

What great times Barbara and I had with the Petteys in their home and at our favorite Cajun seafood restaurant! I often pressed Ron for his opinion of my own mission in life. In prayer, he heard one word: *Continue!* So, I have continued to coach well past the normal retirement years, and share my faith with my athletes and their families. The

Lord granted me the honor of seeing my twenty-eighth national champion in pole vault this summer.

Deuce: I was only one year old the first time you and Ron met me and my family. Friends had asked you to come to the hospital to pray for me. From a chromosome birth defect, I had no immune system—my condition of SCIDS was known as the "bubble boy disease!"

Glenda: Yes, Deuce! Meeting you as an infant began our long relationship with you and your parents, praying for you all along the way.

Deuce: My mom filled many journals recording the stream of miracles that we experienced throughout my young years. Ron predicted several months in advance that we would hear the doctor say: "He's a normal kid!" Those were my doctor's exact words!

Glenda: Yes! After that we came to your T-ball games, birthday parties and any number of regular activities. We loved hearing your mom report that you prayed, "God, fix it!" for other patients when you were only two years old!

Deuce: Mom told me I did that! And . . . God fixed what I asked!

Glenda: You constantly amazed us and confounded the doctors. We are so proud of you—the fine, young man you have grown to be!

Larry: I've been Ron's friend since 2004, and I have witnessed so many people affected by Ron and Glenda's testimony and touch that it is impossible to recall them all. As I mentioned earlier, I believe that the greater good was hope being restored. The goodness of God, as the Father, Son and Holy Spirit, were made real, which opened the entire Word of God to become more personal. I enjoyed being around Ron and to feel the love that came through him and flowed to everyone, especially those in need. There are times I have been in low places in my life and have gone to see Ron, and just a look from my friend seemed to drain away the weight. This very thing happened at their annual Christmas gathering in 2015 at their house. Just seeing Ron smile, even though he was in a wheelchair, brought me such peace. I sat on the hearth of the fireplace just to be near him. The love and peace of the Holy Spirit's presence was so strong on me that I was overwhelmed and could not fight back my tears. Ron Pettey is an example of what God will do through a surrendered person who is open to His Will. I miss him dearly.

Glenda: I want to lighten the mood and share that laughter permeated our relationship from our courtship throughout our marriage. Eventually we understood the spiritual truth that the joy of the Lord is our strength! Through Ron's brain surgeries and subsequent health struggles, the Lord undergirded us with His grace and spirit of joy. No other way could we have survived these circumstances.

A few random moments that Ron and I had in recent years may cause you to smile and even laugh out loud, as I did!

At the end of a long day, as we were both trying to drift off to sleep, Ron said, "Glenda, stop thinking . . . your mind is so loud I can't sleep!"

"What? You're hearing my thoughts?"

"Yes! Now, stop thinking and go to sleep!"

Another night, we were in bed, lights out.

"Ron, I'm sorry to ask you, but could you please pray for my lower back? I'm in too much pain to sleep."

"Sure, Glenda."

"Thanks, so I'll get up and turn on the light."

"No need. I can see just fine."

"What? You can see in the dark?"

"Yes, but it's not dark; your back is perfectly highlighted, totally lit. I can see it just fine." In mere seconds as Ron prayed, my pain was gone.

Several times we were given Music Soaking CDs and Scripture CDs as encouragement for healing. After a few minutes of listening to either the scripture reading or music, Ron would say, "Can we turn that off now?"

"Why, hon? It's very nice and everyone recommends it. I'll turn down the volume."

"It's interfering with what I'm hearing." (The sounds of Heaven!)

Stunned and speechless, I turned it off.

Pam: I feel we all agree that Ron helped countless people through his ministry which lives on today! Ron is now enjoying perfect health and complete joy in Heaven!

Glenda: Yes! Several of my friends have had quick glimpses or dreams of Ron in his younger, healthy body in Heaven, though I have not. Someone warned that writing this book could be sad, but in reality, it has been a joy. Ron's great humility made this book possible only **after** his promotion to Heaven. The legacy of God's work through Ron is our Divine Inheritance.

(From top to bottom:) Ron with one year old Deuce. Rooting for Deuce at his T-Ball Game. Deuce, an honor student in 2016.

CHAPTER SEVENTEEN

THE EPILOGUE

*H*eaven is Real . . . The Rest of the Story respectfully closes with the transcript from the eulogy given by Bob Flournoy at Ron's memorial service March 14, 2016.

Bob Flournoy knew Ron and our entire family as well as anyone could. We thrived attending the Thursday Night Bible Study at his home for two decades, 1992-2012. Bob took a major role in helping us write our first book, which began as a pocket brochure. Bob is our personal attorney. His wife, Genie, is a great friend. What a tearful surprise for me at Ron's memorial when Bob handed me a scroll of the conclusion to this book.

Epilogue by Bob Flournoy

Ron went away for the second and final time on March 14, 2016. As Ron's friend, brother, confidant and partner in pursuit of the Lord, I can only wonder how many lives have been impacted positively by Ron Pettey's first death.

I am sure that Glenda and her family were praying for Ron's full recovery in 1982, but it didn't happen. He survived, but without his memory for ten years. Who could have known that God was preparing him during that time for an extraordinary mission? Not only was He preparing Ron, but also Glenda and their church family, to deliver a testimony that defied all natural thinking and reason. God gave him, and us, a compelling story and experience about the reality of God. But more than that, He was preparing Ron and Glenda to become vessels of truth and hope.

When I first met Ron and Glenda in 1992, his memory had returned in a miraculous way. That was as inexplicable as his experience in Heaven. Everyone knew he was in a memory coma for ten years and undeniably gained it back in an instant, but that gave credibility to all of us that his vivid memory of Heaven was real!

I admit I was a skeptic until I got to know the whole story, even though his memory mirrored what I believed the Word of God taught. Like Thomas, I wanted to see some proof. It turned out that the proof was the messenger himself. Like Nicodemus said of Jesus, "He could not do the things he did but God be with him."

God, who created the universe, chose a very frail individual to be the recipient of information and power through an experience that few people on Earth have ever lived to tell about. Ron was able to recall his time in Heaven *in order* for others to know that Heaven is real—that God does grant eternity with Him to those who know Him personally.

God sovereignly chose Ron and Glenda (as his wife) and endowed them with God's very own presence in a tangible way. God knew Ron would be obedient, even unto death, to lay hands on the sick and see them recover, to proclaim the righteousness and power of God, and to declare this time as an acceptable time for the Lord to show forth His goodness and mercy.

Ron had such an intimate and abiding relationship with the Lord that he had supernatural vision into the generally invisible world of the spirit. He regularly saw angels and ministering spirits that most of us never saw physically. I certainly didn't, but I didn't need to because Ron was the testimony of the Lord to me.

With Ron, no issue was too big or too impossible to pray for because he had his eyes set on the greatness of God. Did everyone he prayed for get healed? Probably not, but they were all affected positively for the glory of God.

I personally saw too many miraculous things happen when Ron spoke the Word of God or extended his hand in the name of the Lord to ever doubt that this was a man sent from God. It reminds me of what was said of King David, that "He was a man that served the purposes of God in his generation and then died."

We are all the beneficiaries of Ron's life and death and second life and death. His mark was indelible on all of us here assembled and literally thousands that we will not know until we are where he is today. Ron is home now and we can only pray that our journey might, even in small measure, be as fruitful as his.

One final thing. We must acknowledge the grace, patience and commitment that Glenda bore to see the testimony of the Lord fulfilled through Ron's experience. She was certainly a vessel of honor—without whom we may never have heard this story, and Ron could have died in vain. She spoke for him when he could not speak—she took him places he could not go alone, and she recognized opportunities that were not always apparent to him. She was a faithful student of the Word of God and trusted in Jesus' prayer when He prayed over his disciples that God might make them one, even as He and God were one. Glenda saw her mission as one that required unity of purpose, empowered by the love of God to good works.

Thank you, Glenda and children, for sharing this extraordinary and supernatural moment in time with all of us. We will never be the same since you welcomed our intrusion into your lives.

I can only imagine the expression of joy on Ron's face when he heard either an angel or the Lord Himself say, "Come in, Ron. We were expecting you—you are right on time!"

ABOUT THE AUTHORS

Glenda Pettey is the co-author with her late husband of their autobiography, Heaven is Real . . . One Man's Journey to Heaven and Back. From Ron's brush with death during brain surgery in 1982 and throughout the eighteen years of the original book's circulation, the couple has encouraged thousands through print, television, radio and speaking to audiences across America and Canada.

Glenda has degrees in English and Counseling with a teaching background. She has published articles in several magazines in print and online. Their story is featured in Modern Day Miracles, Chapter 21, by Amazon best-selling author, Allison Restagno. Glenda, along with her husband Ron, were guests on Sid Roth's "It's Supernatural!," "100 Huntley Street" in Canada, and "Houston Celebration, Daystar," along with local TV and radio. "The 700 Club" filmed the reenactment of the miraculous return of Ron's memory in 1994. In addition to church and ministry events, Glenda and Ron most enjoyed sharing their story on a state university campus which included lively Q and A sessions.

Glenda speaks to Women's groups, conferences and churches, articulating the good news of the gospel with many insights from their life-story. Prepare to stretch as you embrace "with God, nothing is impossible."

Heaven is Real . . . The Rest of the Story could read as fiction if not for the many who knew Ron personally and contribute their own narratives. You will want to read, re-read and share ". . . The Rest of the Story" with its timeless message of Heaven and spiritual truths.

CPSIA information can be obtained
at www.ICGtesting.com
Printed in the USA
LVOW03s1722120617
537831LV00013B/1472/P